CONTENTS

Being Professional

SUCCESS SECRETS

A Common Sense Guide to Lifelong Achievement

by
Merrill Douglass

Honor Books
Tulsa, Oklahoma

Success Secrets
A Common Sense Guide to Lifelong Achievement
ISBN 1-56292-189-4
Copyright by Merrill Douglass
1401 Johnson Ferry Road, Suite 328
Marietta, Georgia 30062

Published by Honor Books, Inc.
P. O. Box 55388
Tulsa, Oklahoma 74155

ABOUT THIS BOOK

Excellence is never achieved in one giant step, but emerges one small step at a time. If you're like me, you're always eager for a new thought or strategy that will prod you to take those steps in the right direction. The purpose of this book is to provide those motivating ideas. Perhaps the ideas presented herein will become important milestones in your effort to grow and succeed.

For several years my column, "Success Secrets," has been a regular feature of the *Christian Management Report*. Many readers have written to tell me they value it for its practical insights and ideas. Some have said it's like having a mentor you respect and admire to help you along the way. Such praise is both gratifying and humbling.

The following pages are a collection of my best columns, selected by the Editorial Staff of the *Christian Management Report*. Most have been previously published in the *Christian Management Report*.

The book is about how to succeed in the business of life. It's about how to be a better person, both on the job and off. My own philosophy of life is the thread which weaves the following articles together. I write about my dreams, my beliefs, my experiences, and my observations. Whether you agree or disagree with me, it is my hope that these articles will make you think. The more our minds grapple with certain issues, the more we know and understand our own opinion and the stronger we become.

God created each of us for greatness. My prayer is that this book will help you to catch a glimpse of your potential and inspire you to strive for the excellence God has planned for your life.

Getting Ahead

Managing Better

Managing Stress

Meet the Author

MANAGING TIME

*There is a time for everything, and a
season for every activity under heaven.*
Ecclesiastes 3:1

1

TIME IS A PARADOX

Time is a paradox. The paradox is, we never seem to have enough time, yet we have all the time there is. Many of us wish we had more time, and we dream of the day when we will have time for all the things we would like to do. We all have exactly the same number of hours in a day, yet some of us are able to produce more with those hours.

The problem, then, is not a shortage of time, but how we choose to use the time available. We need to stop wishing for more time and start learning how to make smarter choices about how we use our time. We will have more time for the things we would like to do when we learn to spend our time wisely.

Most of our choices are made unconsciously because they have become habits. Therefore, in order to make better choices we need to learn more about our habits. Our habits control the vast majority of what we do. The difficulty lies in the fact that we often don't even realize what our habits are.

Habits are learned behaviors. They are things we have repeated so often, they have become the normal, natural, automatic thing to do. We probably didn't purpose to make these behaviors habits, but simply repeating them over and over again causes them to become such. It doesn't require conscious thought; the subconscious mind becomes programmed to do certain things and respond in certain ways.

Once we form habits, they control everything we do until we replace them with new ones. The key is to *purpose* to replace our bad habits with good ones, but we must first know what our habits are.

To learn what our habits are, we must study and analyze our behavior patterns. We might want to ask other people what they notice about our habits. We might keep a journal to record how we respond in certain situations and the choices we make. We can begin to notice a pattern of behavior as we begin to become aware of our actions.

WE NEED TO STOP WISHING FOR MORE TIME AND START LEARNING HOW TO MAKE SMARTER CHOICES.

While positive change may not be easy, it is always worthwhile. When we take time to examine ourselves closely, pinpoint the habits to be changed, and then take the necessary steps to change them, we will begin to make more effective use of our time. We will have learned how to make wise choices.

2

WHERE DOES THE DAY GO?

According to a study by the University of Michigan, the average American adult spends their day as follows: eight hours sleeping, eight hours working, two hours eating, two hours commuting, and one hour on personal hygiene. That leaves about three hours a day for all the other things that make life worth living. By the time you begin to enjoy those things it's bedtime again.

But wait a minute, let's extend this to a week. You only work five days a week. Since you don't work on the weekend, you should have an extra twenty hours plus the usual three hours a day, or about 35 hours each week to enrich your life. That sounds a little better, doesn't it?

Remember, however, these numbers are based on an average forty-hour work week. Many people work more than that. Managers, for example, average about fifty hours a week and executives average almost sixty.

These figures also ignore illness, which will average about five hours a week over your lifetime. And, of course, there is time spent watching TV, which averages over 26 hours weekly for most adults.

When you add it all up, you don't have much time at all. After you do all the things you have to do, there is very little time left over for what you want to do. Plus, if you are not careful, you will waste much of the leftover time.

Good time management is not just an issue for work; it is an issue for all of life. To spend your time is to spend your life; to waste your time is to waste your life. To spend your time wisely is to spend more time doing the things you enjoy.

> GOOD TIME MANAGEMENT IS NOT JUST AN ISSUE FOR WORK; IT IS AN ISSUE FOR ALL OF LIFE.

3

DEADLINES CAN BE GOOD FRIENDS

D o you wait until a deadline is on top of you before you really get moving on a project? Do you do too many things at the last minute? Most of us are guilty on both counts. It is probably a habit that goes back to our early childhood. Left to themselves, almost all school children do their homework at the last possible moment. The same is also true in high school, college, and even graduate school.

When I was a college professor, it always amazed me how the quality of reports varied little, regardless of the time allowed to prepare them. Students would turn in about the same quality of work whether they had two days or two weeks to complete the assignment. No matter how much time they were allowed, most students waited until the last minute anyway.

For most of us, this habit was reinforced through many years of schooling. And truthfully, it did not make much difference during our school years. However, it can make a big difference later on in life.

If you have this tendency, what can you do? First of all, make sure a deadline is set for every project and then honor the deadline. Without a deadline, the last minute never seems to arrive. After setting a deadline, don't just casually set it aside, or you may destroy your credibility with others, and more importantly, with yourself. You will also be developing the disastrous habit of being motivated only when faced with externally imposed deadlines. This habit will almost certainly compound the problem.

WHEN YOU SET DEADLINES, YOU ARE WORKING WITH YOUR HABIT INSTEAD OF AGAINST IT.

When you set deadlines, you are working with your habit instead of against it. Whether the deadline is set by you or someone else, as it approaches you will begin to get in gear. To set a deadline, consider when the project is due, who may be required to work on it after you, and when you will need to be free to begin new projects. If you need to start sooner, simply set the deadline earlier.

Set deadlines and honor them. You will soon find you have mastered an important secret to increased productivity. You will become known as, "The one to give a project to if you want it done on time," rather than "The one who never finishes anything on time." You will be able to get more done without extending your work hours. Deadlines *can* be good friends.

4

QUALITY TIME

D o you sometimes worry about whether or not you are really spending quality time with your children?

It can be a tough dilemma. We love our children, but we are often so busy that it is hard to spend much time with them at all. As a result, we are more concerned than ever with "quality" time.

The truth is, schedules today just don't allow as much quantity time as they used to. Therefore, we would like to maintain as much quality as possible. Here are three guidelines from Gloria Gilbert's book, *2001 Hints for Working Mothers*, which can direct you in your quest for quality time.

Quality time, she says, is any activity that shows your children you are interested in them, care about them, and love them. To decide if an activity qualifies, consider these three questions:

1. Does it involve active participation by both children and parents?

2. Does it draw the family closer together and help foster a sense of self-worth in your children?

3. Does it produce a feeling of happiness and satisfaction for everyone?

That said, in our quest for "quality" time, some of us are really only kidding ourselves to soothe a guilty conscience. What we really need to do is to cut back on our busyness and simply spend more time with our children. Many of us believe we can make up in quality time what we miss in quantity time, but is this true?

There is a lot to be said for just being there. Prudence Mackintosh observed in her book, *Retreads*, "The quality is only apparent when viewed against the vast stretches of quantity. There is a depth in relationships (the quality) that is only possible when you spend quantity time together."

WHAT WE REALLY NEED TO DO IS CUT BACK ON OUR BUSYNESS AND SIMPLY SPEND MORE TIME WITH OUR CHILDREN.

So you can see, quality alone is not enough. While you follow Gloria Gilbert's guidelines to increase quality, also concentrate on "just being there." Your kids are only with you for a brief time — don't miss it!

5

SPEAK UP TO AVOID TIME PRESSURES

Pressure often comes from realizing that you have too much to do and not enough time to do it. If you are feeling pressed for time, what can you do about it?

All of us fall prey to this condition at one time or another. Some of us seem to be in this squeeze every day. Getting into it is easy; getting out is tough.

One of the primary causes of time pressure is our inability to say no. Saying no can be difficult, almost impossible for some. It is hard for nonassertive people to say no even when they realize it is the best response. It is hard for most of us to say no when the boss is asking, even when we know our failure to say no creates time pressures.

I have talked with hundreds of people who work 70, 80, even 90 hours a week. Very few of them enjoy working that many hours.

Many of them feel their company takes advantage of them. Yet they seldom stop to consider that they may have brought the situation upon themselves.

Suppose your boss comes by one afternoon and asks you to tackle another special project. You respond, "Yes, sir. I'll get on it right away." The boss goes away happy, believing that all is well.

What you should have said is, "Wait a minute, boss. I'd really love to do that, but do you realize everything I'm already doing? Which tasks do you want me to set aside in order to tackle this new assignment?" If you are really loaded up and you fail to say so, you are contributing to your own demise.

ONE OF THE PRIMARY CAUSES OF TIME PRESSURE IS OUR INABILITY TO SAY NO.

The boss should know how loaded up we are without us having to say anything, we reason. That would be nice, but it is unrealistic. Truth is, many bosses won't ever know unless you tell them or until you fail to deliver results on time. Learning about a problem early on is always better than hearing about it after the fact.

Speak up. Honestly evaluate your work load and say no when necessary. No one performs at their best when they are feeling the time pressure that comes from being over-committed.

6

JUST A MINUTE

D o you ever think about how short life is?

If you do, you are probably over 40. Or perhaps some special circumstance has forced you to think about it. I qualify on both counts. I am over 40, and I just returned from a friend's funeral.

Even the average life-span of 80 years is but a breath compared to eternity, and that's an average. This means some lives are cut short for one reason or another and some people live much longer. For my friend, it was a sudden heart attack. It could have been anything. The cause and the timing are the only uncertain things about death. The certainty is that it will come.

For some reason, my friend's funeral caused me to think about a phrase that is used daily in our house, especially by my daughters. Ask them to do something and they will probably say, "In a minute." "Wait a minute until I get to the end of the chapter." "Just a minute, wait until this show's over."

It occurred to me that we would probably like to say "Wait a minute," when death beckons. "Just a minute, wait until I get to the end of the year." "In a minute; my daughter hasn't finished college yet." "Just a minute; I need more time to accomplish something with my life."

Our eternity beyond death will be very different from our life. Things that seemed so important will no linger be meaningful. What has worked before won't work any longer. Other people may wait for us, but death does not. When your time is up, it's up. Whether you were ready for it or not is beside the point. Your unfinished projects will remain unfinished forever. Your postponed intentions will be eternally postponed.

LIFE IS VERY SHORT AND THERE'S NO WAY TO FILE FOR AN EXTENSION.

When you think about it, life is very short and there's no way to file for an extension. Doesn't it make sense, then, to spend more of your time on the really important things? Then when death comes for you, you won't have to say, "Just a minute." You will have used your minutes well.

SORTING MAIL REDUCES PAPERWORK

D o you really throw away junk mail without opening it or do you take a peek, just out of curiosity? An envelope never opened is paper you never have to handle. The first line of defense in the war against paper is to toss out as much as you can without even opening it.

Knowing what to open and what to throw out is easier than you may think. There are clues all over the envelope that can help you decide. For instance, look at the return address, or the lack thereof. Check the postage rate. Is it bulk rate or first class? Notice how the postage is stamped. Is it metered or a real stamp? The color, type, and size of the envelope, as well as how much is stuffed into it, are other helpful clues.

Is the envelope addressed to you or to someone else? Is your name spelled correctly and your proper title (Mr. or Mrs.) used? Was it addressed with a label, typewriter, computer, or was it handwritten? Read everything printed on the outside of the envelope. Just by paying attention to all the clues, you can probably throw away a significant percentage of your mail and be done with it within seconds.

You will also need a good sorting system when you begin to open the remaining mail. Start with these three basic groups: action, information, and reading. Add other categories as needed. For instance, you may want to divide action paper into urgent and non-urgent.

Action paper includes anything that requires you to do something. Keep it separate so you can handle it quickly. The information category is for those things you need to know daily. The reading category is for all materials you want to read, like magazines or reports. If there is quite a lot of reading material, you may want to sort it into specific categories, such as: magazines, newsletters, or company reports.

THE FIRST LINE OF DEFENSE IN THE WAR AGAINST PAPER IS TO TOSS OUT AS MUCH AS YOU CAN WITHOUT EVEN OPENING IT.

A systematic approach — not just a haphazard approach — to sorting mail makes responding to it much easier. Schedule time for action paper first, then information paper, and finally, reading paper.

Use the clues to detect the junk mail, and throw it out. Sort what remains into categories based on your needs. Finally, determine the priority status of each category and schedule your time accordingly. Using this approach will reduce your war on paper to an occasional skirmish.

8

STAND UP TO GET MORE DONE

D id you know that standing up can help improve your performance? Standing has more virtues than most of us realize. It is one of the most overlooked secrets to getting more done during the day.

Take interruptions, for example. Have you ever noticed how much longer they seem to take when people sit down? Think about it. Most of us sit when we go to talk to someone. What might happen if you stood up when someone dropped in to see you? If you don't sit down, they probably won't either. It would be a breach of etiquette. They will probably get to the point quicker and be on their way. Then you can sit down and get back to your work.

Standing up might even improve your relationships with others. Here is a common example: Someone pops into your office. You don't even stop writing or lift your eyes from your desk, but tell them you are listening and to go ahead. Have you ever thought about the message you have just given that person? If you stand up when they enter, you would automatically give them your full attention. The nonverbal message you send will be much more positive and you will save time as well.

Consider the impact of having a stand-up meeting. You will probably get much more done in far less time. The mere act of standing changes the expectations about the meeting. Some companies have used stand-up conference tables and discovered people love them.

STANDING PUTS YOU IN A BETTER POSITION TO TAKE ACTION.

Standing helps in other ways too. For instance, standing can be a status or power equalizer. Most people consider standing to be more formal than sitting. Standing puts you in a better position to take action. Some people claim they think better when standing.

Why not experiment with standing yourself? You will probably discover many ways that standing can help you save time.

SCHEDULING TIPS

Jim McCay wrote, "Nothing ever happens until you create the space for it to happen in." Creating the space for something to happen in means scheduling a specific time for it. When you schedule an activity, you automatically increase the probability that it will happen. Here are four tips which can help you become a better scheduler.

1. Always write out your schedule. A mental note won't work for most of us. Too many things are happening. The day is fragmented, and we're pushed and pulled in several directions at once. What we think we'll remember is soon crowded out of our mind by the tyranny of the urgent.

2. Once you've written out your schedule, check it frequently. Look at your monthly schedule at least once a week. Check your weekly schedule once or twice a day and your daily schedule at least

once an hour. Continual review of your schedule will keep your mind focused, which helps you stay on track.

3. Be sure to allot enough time for things, but not too much time. Parkinson's Law says that work expands to fill the time allowed. Most of us underestimate how much time we'll need for a task, so we add more time to the estimate, just in case. Trouble is, it's easy to go too far the other way and allow too much time. That's when Parkinson's Law takes over. The key to avoiding it is a realistic estimate, not too much and not too little.

WHEN YOU SCHEDULE AN ACTIVITY, YOU AUTOMATICALLY INCREASE THE PROBABILITY THAT IT WILL HAPPEN.

4. When you can, match your work to your body's cycles. For instance, if you are a morning person, you are at your best early in the day. Try to fill your morning with things that are more critical, or those that require careful thought or creativity. If you're an afternoon person, your mental powers peak later in the day. You'll want to shift the creative, critical items to later in the day.

However you arrange your schedule, pay attention to what works well for you and what doesn't. At the end of the day, examine the difference between what you actually did versus what you had planned to do. Before long you'll know how to best schedule your time to get the best results.

10

TACKLING TELEPHONE TAG

Does playing telephone tag frustrate you?

You know how the game goes. You call me, but I'm not there, so you leave a message for me to call you back. But when I call you back, you're not there, or you're tied up and can't take the call, so I leave a message for you to call me again. These calls can bounce back and forth for hours, days — even weeks.

There are several things you can do to cut down on telephone tag. For instance, if the person you're calling is out, perhaps someone else can help you. If not, try setting up a specific telephone appointment rather than simply leaving a message.

Most of us have certain times when we're more likely to be reached. I call these preferred call times. Informing frequent callers of those times can also help cut down on phone tag. Ask others for theirs as well. Some people now list the best times to call them right on their business cards.

Sometimes voice mail or answering machines can help. As much as we may dislike them, they enable you to be in two places at once. I once concluded a business deal solely through messages back and forth on our answering machines.

Carrying electronic beepers may also help reduce telephone tag. The newer models even display a digital message as well as an audible beep.

Many telephone systems accommodate call forwarding. Calls to your phone number can be automatically forwarded to wherever you are, whether you're across the hall, in your car, or even across the country.

Electronic mail (e-mail) and message services are other alternatives to telephone contact. Using computer modems, you can converse with anyone, regardless of time schedules.

SOME PEOPLE NOW LIST THE BEST TIMES TO CALL THEM RIGHT ON THEIR BUSINESS CARDS.

Telephone tag. You may never eliminate it, but by using the above suggestions you can certainly reduce it.

11

HOW CEOs SPEND THEIR TIME

According to a recent study, CEOs typically work 10 to 12 hours daily, plus 10 or so hours on the weekend. They also start the day early, usually around 6:30 a.m. So what do they do to make those hours the most productive they can be? How do they manage their time?

Delegation is a must. One CEO stated, "There is always more to do than there is time to do it. I am constantly adjusting my priorities to accomplish what is most important, and delegating those areas that are less important. However, I must have specific objectives and plans so I can determine my priorities."

The CEOs in the study also pointed out that having a good secretary helps them spend their time wisely. In addition, they said good telecommunications and effective information systems are important. Cellular telephones are a common tool for CEOs.

Staying away from nonessential work was another helpful strategy mentioned. CEOs try to attend to only the important issues and let assistants handle the details.

Most CEOs require firm agendas for meetings, set tight daily calendars, and schedule business meetings during breakfast and lunch.

Like the rest of us, CEOs often wish they had more time for certain issues. Organizational and human resource development are the two areas that most agreed need more attention than they are able to give.

CEOs USUALLY DEVELOP THESE SKILLS LONG BEFORE THEY BECOME CEOs.

Delegation, planning, setting priorities, staying away from trivial work, and setting tight agendas are useful skills that can help anyone. In fact, CEOs usually develop these skills long before they become CEOs. In other words, good time management skills will not only help you get more done, they may also help you get promoted.

12

DEVELOPING PRIORITIES

Have you ever been a "C" priority?

Many years ago, when my wife was a freshman at Indiana University, she was starry-eyed over a handsome fraternity boy she called Hank. Many an important quiz, paper, or exam were sacrificed to the hours she spent daydreaming about Hank, not to mention the time she spent doing his laundry! Besides being one good-looking guy, Hank was also very clever. To this day, he is the only man who ever convinced her to iron his shirts!

One afternoon Hank arrived at her dorm to pick up the eight shirts he had left a few days earlier. She smiled and proudly handed over his freshly pressed duds, then invited him to have a coke with her. Her smile fumed to dismay when she heard his response to her invitation.

"Sweetheart," he said, "I like you a lot, but there are 10,000 girls on campus, and I only have so much time!" Handsome Hank grabbed his shirts and walked out of her life. Although it was a lucky break for me, for her it was an abrupt introduction to being a "C" priority.

Priorities! When there are so many great things to do, how do you decide which things are most important?

To determine your priorities, examine your goals. Next to each of your written goal statements, note the importance of each goal by giving it an "A," "B," or "C." An "A" means the goal is very important to you. "B" means the goal is moderately important to you. And "C" means the goal is not really that important.

TO DETERMINE YOUR PRIORITIES, EXAMINE YOUR GOALS.

Now for the hard part. Read over each of your "A" goals and rank them according to their relative importance. Label the most important goal "1," the second "2," and so on. When this task is finished, you will have a priority system for your goals.

A simple task? Of course not. But the alternative — not accomplishing anything — is much worse. By forcing yourself to make some tough choices, you are on the road to reaching your goals. You are meeting your life head on and making the best of what you have. You can ask no more of yourself.

13
DEADLINES

D o you love deadlines, or do you dread them?

We know deadlines tend to get us moving as they draw near; but for many of us, this kind of pressure carries a negative connotation. It would be better if we could learn to look at the positive benefits of deadlines.

For example, a deadline changes your project from a nebulous maybe to a definite reality. Of course, this greatly improves the chances that things will actually get done, maybe even done on time. Can you imagine how much tax revenue the government would collect if there were no specific deadlines for payment?

Deadlines help counter Parkinson's Law: Work tends to expand to fill the time available for its accomplishment. If you have all day to do something, it will probably take all day to get it done. If you have only an hour or two, you will do it much earlier. That is one big reason why projects should not have open-ended dates.

Tell people to drop by sometime, and you will never see them. Ask them to come by next Friday at 8:00 p.m. and they probably will. The result of this type of specific deadline is that you will see your friends more often.

Deadlines also force you to plan better. They automatically cause you to think about what has to be done, how long each part will take, and when the best or most logical starting time would be. Do this often enough, and you will develop a new way of thinking. You will find it easier to muster the self-discipline necessary to accomplish more in less time. As a result, your personal productivity will increase and you will become a more valuable worker.

A DEADLINE CHANGES YOUR PROJECT FROM A NEBULOUS MAYBE TO A DEFINITE REALITY.

The next time you are moaning about deadlines, stop for a minute and think about the valuable benefits those deadlines have to offer!

14

GOOD HABITS HELP

Do your habits help you achieve positive results, or do they hinder your success? Check your habits against these good time-management habits.

Habit No. 1: Keep setting new goals. The simple truth is that people who regularly write out their goals achieve more. Studies show they also make more money and gain more personal fulfillment.

Habit No. 2: Analyze your behavior. What do you do? Why do you do it? How often do you do it? How much time do you spend doing it? How much does it help? At least once a year, keep a time log for a month. Track both work time and personal time.

Habit No. 3: Plan your time. A good plan will help you accomplish more. It will also save you time and effort. Write out a plan for every week. What are your goals for this week? What must you do? When will different activities take place? How much time will you need? Try this for several weeks, and then evaluate your progress to see how much it helps.

Habit No. 4: Cut out timewasters. Most of us complain about the timewasters in our lives. However, very few people are actively working to eliminate the timewasters that bother them most. Stop complaining and take action. Pick one timewaster every week, and focus on decreasing it. Can you eliminate it? Can you reduce it? Can you lessen its impact? Do this every week, all year long. In just a few weeks, you will have formed the habit of searching for and eliminating timewasters.

IT IS MUCH EASIER TO ACHIEVE RESULTS WHEN YOUR HABITS WORK WITH YOU RATHER THAN AGAINST YOU.

Habit No. 5: Stop procrastinating. We often try to side-step unpleasant things by putting them off. Sometimes it works; most of the time it doesn't. Fight the do-it-later urge. Do it now instead.

It is much easier to achieve results when your habits work with you rather than against you. Master these five good time habits, and you will have time on your side.

15

HOW TO CONQUER PROCRASTINATION

The two most prevalent reasons for procrastination are unpleasantness and complexity. Unpleasant tasks are the worst of the two and, therefore, create the biggest problem. Ironically, the longer we put off doing these tasks, the more unpleasant they become. However, once we get started, we sometimes discover a task is not nearly as bad as we thought it was going to be!

When facing an unpleasant task, try these ideas.

1. Do the toughest jobs first. Get them out of the way early.

2. Analyze the task. Why do you dread it? Directly confront the distasteful part.

3. Tackle the task in bits and pieces. Cut it down into segments you can do a few minutes at a time.

4. Set a deadline for yourself.

5. Promise others that you will complete the task by a specific time.

6. Reward yourself for finishing the task.

7. Have someone else do the task for you.

8. Consider the cost of delaying, and the benefit of acting now.

Complexity is the second major reason for procrastinating. Some tasks appear overwhelming; we don't know what to do, or even where to start. Or, we may not be in the mood to tackle something so complex right now.

To get beyond the fear of complexity, try these ideas.

THE TWO MOST PREVALENT REASONS FOR PROCRASTINATION ARE UNPLEASANTNESS AND COMPLEXITY.

1. Break the task down into small steps.

2. Focus on one step at a time.

3. Break the steps down further, into several "mini-jobs" that can be completed in ten or fifteen minutes.

4. Don't wait for the right mood; start now. Talk yourself into starting any way you can. Instead of thinking you're not in the mood to do it, tell yourself how good you will feel when you're done.

No matter what causes the do-it-later urge — whether unpleasantness or complexity — the ideas listed above can help you overcome it with do-it-now action.

16

BUNCH INTERRUPTIONS TO GET MORE DONE

I t would be easy to get more done if only you could cut down on interruptions. How? A major step is to bunch interrupting items together.

Most of us interrupt others in a haphazard manner. We call or drop-in whenever we think of it. Our focus is on what we are doing, what we need, what we are trying to avoid. We seldom stop to think about what this constant barrage does to others. Nonetheless, we often complain about what their constant interruptions do to us.

Some interruptions are important, but most are merely routine or completely unnecessary. Timing is not critical for most routine matters. They may need to be done, but it doesn't have to be right now. Therefore, we could bunch several of these routine matters together and handle them all at one time.

If everyone would bunch their routine items like this, we could solve about half the interruption problems in this country immediately. Here are several ways others do it that might work for you too.

Some people keep a notebook with one name per page. They write topics they need to discuss with someone on their page. Periodically, they call or meet with each person to go over the accumulated items. One good technique is to write your question or comment on the left side of the page. Then, use the right side of the page to note their replies.

Some people prefer to collect items in file folders, boxes, trays, or even wall pocket files. Whenever they think of something to see a particular person about, they make a note of it and put in the file folder designated for that person.

One creative person used a white board and dry-erase markers. He divided the board into several grids and assigned one name per grid. He made notes in the grids. When he called to discuss the items, he erased them as they were covered. When he had erased all the items, he said good-bye. You could also use a bulletin board with thumbtacks or push pins to hold notes under different groups.

SOME INTERRUPTIONS ARE IMPORTANT, BUT MOST ARE MERELY ROUTINE OR COMPLETELY UNNECESSARY.

Start with the ideas here and find what works best for you. Whatever method you decide to use, if used consistently you will find you get much more done in the uninterrupted times. Then you'll be able to handle the normally routine interruptions much more efficiently and effectively.

17

QUIET TIME INCREASES PRODUCTIVITY

Most people who work in offices find their days frantic, fragmented, and frustrating. An endless stream of interruptions makes it difficult to get things done. The constant start-stop-restart pattern stretches tasks out longer than necessary and often reduces the quality of the work. Many people seem to accomplish only about half of what they should be able to do in a work day. Quiet time can change all this.

Quiet time is simple: You create an uninterrupted block of time so you can concentrate on your work. This usually means turning off the telephone and blocking drop-in visitors for awhile.

What should you do during quiet time? Think; plan; get organized. Do analytical work, write reports, or work on projects that require creativity. One big plus is that in one hour of quiet time, you can get as much done as you could in three or four hours of regular time.

Most people these days favor quiet time; they just don't know how to find it. You won't just find it; you have to make it happen. Close your door, turn off your telephone, find an empty conference room, go to the library — do whatever you must.

IN ONE HOUR OF QUIET TIME, YOU CAN GET AS MUCH DONE AS YOU COULD IN THREE OR FOUR HOURS OF REGULAR TIME.

On the other hand, be careful not to abuse the quiet time concept. You can't isolate yourself all day, but most of us can afford to be unavailable for an hour or so once or twice a day. Test it and see for yourself how to make it work best for you. If you are courageous, you can even create group quiet time so lots of people can benefit.

Remember, if you want to increase your productivity without increasing your hours, just make some quiet time for yourself.

18

DECIDING WHAT TO DO

E very day we face an endless stream of work. Phone calls, mail, meetings, superiors, and colleagues all produce more work for us. Sometimes we get it all done. However, on most days, we have more work than we can handle.

One reason we become over-committed is that we don't consider the value of what we are committing to. A second problem is that we often fail to consider how much time we will need to honor all our commitments.

Here are two very practical questions that can help you to keep everything under control. Use these questions to sort out all the potential jobs that come your way.

Question No. 1. Will I do this task? Just because someone asks for it to be done doesn't mean it is worth doing. Will it help accomplish something worthwhile? What would happen if you said no? Are you the one who should be doing it? Don't say yes just to get them off your back. If you answer no to this first question, you will have fewer jobs to do. If you answer yes, then go on to the next question.

Question No. 2. When will I do this task? We often take on too much because we are trying to be helpful. We say yes too easily. If you have agreed to do the task, when will you find the time? If you can't say when, what makes you think you will *ever* find the time to do it? Your yes turns into no after the fact, when you fail to deliver. That is much worse than saying no in the first place.

There are only three realistic answers to this second question. You will either do the task today, one day this month, or one month this year. Once you decide, note it on your calendar, file it accordingly, then complete it at the time scheduled.

For most people, saying yes is easy; deciding when is tough. Just remember, you will never run out of work, but you'll often run out of time. Therefore, never agree to take on a job without first considering *when* you will be able to do it.

ONE REASON WE BECOME OVER-COMMITTED IS WE DON'T CONSIDER THE VALUE OF WHAT WE ARE COMMITTING TO.

19

CHOOSING THE RIGHT NOTEBOOK ORGANIZER

People repeatedly ask me these two questions: Do you recommend using any of the notebook organizer/planner systems? If so, which one do you recommend? The first question is easy — yes, I recommend using them! The second question is more difficult.

There are dozens of planning and organizing systems on the market. Most are useful, although some seem better than others. The best answer for which one to buy is this: Choose the one *you* will use.

The difficulty in recommending one is that I don't know enough about you. Do you want one for your work, your personal life, or both? What size do you prefer? Will you be carrying it around or leaving it on your desk? How many and what kind of activities are you involved in? How many details must you track? What is your predominant work style?

CHOOSING THE RIGHT NOTEBOOK ORGANIZER

For 30 years I've been studying how people work, how they use their time, and how they can work smarter. I've seen just about every planner and organizer there is. The best have eight common elements:

1. A yearly calendar.
2. Monthly calendars.
3. Planning sheets for each day.
4. A telephone and address section.
5. A set of A-Z tabs.
6. A second set of tabs with customizable labels.
7. A variety of specialized forms or worksheets.
8. A sheet for recording notes.

THE DIFFICULTY IN RECOMMENDING ONE IS THAT I DON'T KNOW ENOUGH ABOUT YOU.

Any system that omits one or more of these elements would be suspect. Without these eight elements, the system would not be flexible and, therefore, less useful.

For systems which have all the elements, the next set of criteria concern the daily planning sheets. These sheets should direct you to identify goals and activities, set priorities, estimate time needed for each activity, and schedule specific activities. Many notebook systems omit the time estimates. However, without this you won't know whether or not your plan is realistic — you run out of time, not activities.

Use these guidelines to help sort out the different products and you'll probably pick the one that is right for you.

20

SEVEN TIPS FOR TAMING TELEPHONE TIME

Telephones are a major part of most days, and we spend a lot of time using them. Some of this time spent is rewarding, some is not. To make the time spent more rewarding, develop good telephone habits. The following seven tips can help you do just that.

1. Plan your call before you dial. A recent study found that the average business call was almost 11 minutes. However, the average *planned* call is only 7 minutes. Planning can help you get more done in less time. You will probably get better results too.

2. Ask people you call often when they are most likely to be in and call at those times. Tell them the best time to call you too. Using preferred call times can help reduce telephone tag.

3. When someone answers, give them complete information. For example: "Hello. This is Merrill Douglass. I'm calling Fred

Anderson about our pending contract. Will you please connect us?" This saves time spent answering the inevitable questions. This approach will not only get you connected faster, it will also get you connected more often.

4. Skip the small talk. Telephone calls are interruptions. While you're asking, "How are you?" the person you are calling is wondering what you want. Getting right to the point will save both of you time.

5. Don't leave messages. Few people return calls right away, and many don't return them at all. If it's important, ask when would be the best time to call again.

6. If you must leave a message, be sure it's complete. An AT&T study showed that 97 percent of messages contain only a name and a number. Leaving a complete message increases your chances for a returned call. If the person

PLAN YOUR CALL BEFORE YOU DIAL.

you are calling is not in, someone else may be able to help you. If you have left a complete message, at least the other person can leave you an answer if they get your machine when they call back.

7. Consider alternatives. AT&T recently reported that the chances are only 1 in 6 that you will reach the person you're calling on the first try. It might be better to send a postcard, letter, e-mail, or fax.

As you implement the seven strategies — planning your call; using preferred call times; giving complete information; skipping small talk; eliminating messages; leaving complete messages; and considering alternatives — you will find that you're spending much less time on the phone but actually producing more.

21

USE A MASTER LIST TO MASTER TIME

M ost people make a daily to-do list. The problem, however, is rethinking your list every day. You see your days as independent of one another, rather than interrelated. You rearrange your priorities each time you rethink your list.

A better approach is to create a master list. A master list is simply a list of all the items you need to complete. Add new items to the list as they come up. When you finally complete a task, cross it off the list.

When you fill up an entire page, start a second page. When most of the items on page one are completed, transfer the unfinished ones to page two and discard the older page. For really busy people, a master list could require three or four pages. Be careful, however, if the list grows too long. Chances are, you need to say "no" more often.

To fine-tune your master list, add assignment dates, priority codes, due dates, and time estimates. The assignment date is the date you add the item to your master list. As you move an unfinished item from page to page, the assignment date never changes. As the assignment gets older, you may be procrastinating. Either drop the task or get it done.

Priority codes rank the importance of each item. The priority code is set when you put the item on your master list. This helps you to keep low value junk off the list. It also prevents rethinking your priorities as your moods change.

The due date indicates when the task must be completed. As the due date gets closer, the task becomes more urgent. This applies pressure, which keeps you moving.

Time estimates show how long it will take to do each task. Considering the time estimate and the due date together will tell you when to start. This makes it easier to schedule your work. Paying attention to the logical starting time will also prevent many of those last-minute rush jobs.

USING A MASTER LIST WILL KEEP YOU FOCUSED ON YOUR PRIORITIES, PREVENT PROCRASTINATION, AND HELP YOU PRODUCE MORE IN LESS TIME.

Using a master list will keep you focused on your priorities, prevent procrastination, and help you produce more in less time.

22

HOW TO MAKE MEETINGS PRODUCTIVE

Almost everyone hates to waste time in unproductive meetings. Yet year after year we go right on whittling away time in meetings that produce very little.

For executives and managers, meetings are a major problem. Recent studies show that managers spend an average of 43 percent of the work week in meetings. Executives spend an average of 65 percent of the week in meetings. When asked about the value of meetings, both groups say at least half the meeting time is wasted.

If so much time is wasted in meetings, it would certainly be worth the effort to make an improvement. Here are twelve tips that can help make your meetings more productive.

1. Drop unnecessary meetings. Make sure there is a valid purpose for every meeting.

2. Allow people to come, make their contribution, and leave when they are finished.

3. Make decisions without meetings whenever appropriate, and never use a committee for something that can be done by an individual.

4. Use an agenda and stick to it.

5. Set a time limit, then start and stop on time.

6. Invite only those people you need, and tell them what will be expected of them.

7. Try holding a meeting with everyone standing; see if you can get more done in less time.

8. Cut out the small talk, whether it is yours or someone else's.

9. Spend a few minutes at the end of each meeting to critique its quality.

10. Be prepared for the meeting and stick to its topic.

11. Consider alternatives to meetings — memos, e-mail, conference calls.

GOOD MEETINGS... MUST BE CAREFULLY PLANNED AND SKILLFULLY RUN.

12. Prepare a follow-up plan for distribution at the end of the meeting. Make sure everyone knows who is responsible for which actions and when they are due.

Good meetings will not just happen. They must be carefully planned and skillfully run. The rewards, however, are well worth the effort.

23

HOW TO DEVELOP THE ON-TIME HABIT

Waiting is a part of any job. We wait for people who are late for meetings and appointments. We wait for work that was due but is not finished. We wait for decisions, approvals, or information we need. Too much waiting wastes time, delays results, and destroys relationships.

Some waiting is inevitable and unavoidable. Just accept it and learn to live with it. We could trim much of the wasteful waiting, though, if we would all adopt the on-time habit. Here are six steps that can help.

1. Estimate time needs. How long will it actually take to complete something? Running out of time often results from not considering how much time you really need.

2. Start on time. Don't wait until the last minute. Give yourself plenty of time to do the job right, and finish by the deadline.

3. Set your watch early. Vince Lombardi, legendary coach of the Green Bay Packers football team, told his players if they weren't 15 minutes early, they were late. His players set their watches ahead to make sure they were on time.

4. Focus on leaving time, not arrival time. For example, suppose you must leave by 2:15 to get to a 3:00 meeting. Think 2:15, not 3:00. Focus all your efforts on leaving by 2:15. If you focus on 3:00, you are more likely to be late.

5. Avoid the "one last thing" tendency. When it's time to go, leave. Don't give in to the temptation to take one more call, handle one more question, or write one more memo. Trying to squeeze in one more task will often make you late.

TOO MUCH WAITING WASTES TIME, DELAYS RESULTS, AND DESTROYS RELATIONSHIPS.

6. Allow for the unexpected. Sometimes things go wrong. When you're in a hurry, more things go wrong. Allow extra time in your schedule to handle unexpected problems.

Change your habits. Commit yourself to being an on-time person. You'll love the results!

24

THERE ARE ONLY TWO WAYS TO WASTE TIME

There are only two ways to waste time. One way is to spend it on tasks that aren't necessary. The other way is to spend too much time on the tasks which are necessary. The first makes you ineffective; the second makes you inefficient.

Peter Drucker, the renowned management guru, once wrote, "Most people are more concerned with doing things right, than with doing the right things." Doing things right leads to efficiency, while doing the right things leads to effectiveness. However, it's not just a matter of choosing efficiency or effectiveness. We need both. Therefore, we must do the right things right.

Most people tell us that time management is mostly a matter of doing things in less time. But that's only partly true. Striving to improve efficiency is almost useless until we know what really needs to be done. This requires setting goals, determining our priorities, and developing plans to achieve the goals. There is no point in doing well what doesn't need to be done at all.

Examine your operations closely. Exactly what result are you trying to achieve? What really helps you get that result and what doesn't? What would happen if you discontinued some activities?

Once you've decided what the right things are, analyze them for efficiency. How could you shorten the time span? Could you combine some steps? Could you modify things in some way? How could you get the same result in less time, or fewer steps? Would it help to alter the timing or location of the task? Should jobs be assigned differently?

THERE IS NO POINT IN DOING WELL WHAT DOESN'T NEED TO BE DONE AT ALL.

Get everyone involved in both steps. Conduct brainstorming sessions. Talk to customers and suppliers. Do benchmark comparisons with companies that do similar work excellently. What can you learn from them? Keep accurate time logs and study them carefully. Look for problems that block productivity. Strive to improve both yourself and the system in which you work.

Two ways to waste time are being ineffective and being inefficient. Remember to eliminate ineffectiveness first, then work on inefficiencies. When effectiveness and efficiency work hand-in-hand, they create tremendous results.

25

EVERYONE HAS THREE JOBS

There are three ways to view every job. First, there is your *perceived* job — what you *think* you are doing. Second, there is your *ideal* job — what you *ought* to be doing. And third, there is your *actual* job — what you *are* doing. Examining your job from all three perspectives can provide valuable insight for improving your performance. Here is how to do it.

First, write out a list of everything you do in your job. This is like a brief job description. List everything you can think of.

Next, you will want to consider the value of each segment. Considering the overall results you are responsible for achieving, what is the importance of each item you have listed? How much does each one contribute to your results? Rank everything on your list from the most important to the least important.

Then, estimate what percentage of your time you think you are spending on every item you have listed. Consider a typical week, month, or whatever time frame is easiest for you. Be sure the total equals 100 percent.

You now have your perceived job. To find your ideal job, add any activities to the list which you really ought to be doing, but are not doing at present. Then look over your entire list again. Ask yourself what percentage of your time you should be spending on each item to produce the best overall results. Again, the total must come to 100 percent.

EXAMINING YOUR JOB FROM...THREE PERSPECTIVES CAN PROVIDE VALUABLE INSIGHT FOR IMPROVING YOUR PERFORMANCE.

Finally, to see your actual job, simply keep a record of how you spend your time for a few weeks. Summarize the amount of time you actually spent on each of the items you have listed.

You are now ready to analyze the variances, or differences, between what you think you are doing, what you ought to be doing, and what you are actually doing. You will probably see many ways to improve your time allocations.

This is a powerful exercise. Those who try it almost always find ways to improve their performance and thereby contribute more. Why not try it for yourself? You get a lot of gain for a little effort.

26

TIME LOGS REALLY HELP

D o you really know exactly what you did yesterday, and exactly how much time you spent on each of your activities? What about the day before that? What about last week? Can you actually remember all the details?

Most of us really don't know where our time goes. We can't even recall everything we do, let alone how much time we spend doing it. We desire to manage our time better; however, what we fail to realize is that it is difficult to make improvements when we don't even realize what we're presently spending our time doing.

Facts about time use are easy to get. All you have to do is keep a time log. Use it to record everything you do, when you do it, and how long it takes to do it. Begin your record in the morning, and keep it with you as you go through the day. Keeping the log in front of you will remind you to continue recording activities.

Record your time in 15-minute segments. During some segments you will be doing only one thing — attending a meeting, for instance. During others, you may be doing several things — answering two telephone calls, opening your mail, and instructing a staff person. Don't be concerned about capturing every single activity. Concentrate on the most important ones or those that take the most time.

Record activities as you do them, not all at once at the end of the day. Nobody's memory is that good! Resist the tendency to generalize or make yourself look good on paper. You will only be fooling yourself, and the time invested in analysis will be wasted.

MOST OF US REALLY DON'T KNOW WHERE OUR TIME GOES.

How long should you record your time? There is no standard answer for this question. You should record your time until you believe you have covered a representative period. For some, this may be only two or three days. For others, it may be a month or more.

Time logs are an excellent idea, probably one of the best ways known to help you discover how to use your time better. In fact, all the best time managers regularly analyze their time to discover better ways to use it. If you want to be a top time manager, you would be smart to start with a time log. Why not start yours today?

SETTING GOALS

*Many are the plans in a man's heart,
but it is the Lord's purpose that prevails.
Proverbs 19:21*

27

WHAT SUCCESS MEANS

What is your definition of success? Does it make any difference how you measure success? Do you even need to worry about defining success?

Personal Selling Power, the sales and marketing newsletter, recently conducted a survey among executives. The survey asked them to describe what success meant to them personally. Their responses fell into four categories.

In the first group, success meant owning material possessions, such as houses, cars, or airplanes.

The second group defined success as experiencing particular feelings. For instance, they might strive to feel satisfied or happy.

The third group saw success as achieving goals. To them, success was a process of getting from one point to the next. They set goals, achieved them, then set new goals.

The fourth group believed that success related to their personal mission. They said each of us has some mission in life. Success to them meant finding and fulfilling their mission.

The differences between the four groups are easy to see. However, does it really matter? Experience suggests that the first three groups often run into serious problems. Material possessions never satisfy for long, feelings are nebulous, and even goals can become meaningless after awhile. The people in group four seem to have a deeper foundation. Possessions, feelings, and goals all take on new meaning when measured by a life mission.

DEFINING SUCCESS IS THE FIRST STEP IN ACHIEVING IT.

How you define success for yourself is very important. The survey said that defining success is the first step in achieving it. People who don't have a personal definition for success feel less successful and earn less money. They are also less satisfied with their careers and their lives in general.

If you want to be successful, you must first define what success means to you. But be wary, some definitions will serve you better than others.

28

GOALS ARE ROAD MAPS

I f you were planning to drive somewhere you'd never been before, wouldn't you consult a road map?

For several years, I lived in Los Angeles. What a wild maze of streets and freeways! I never went to a new part of town without checking the map first. Even then, I didn't always have an easy time. But without that map, I didn't have a chance.

Life is the same way. You can wander along never knowing for sure where you're going, or you can set goals and develop plans. Goals and plans are like road maps. They won't guarantee you a smooth trip, but they will tell you the right direction in which to travel. Without them, life is like getting lost in a freeway interchange. You can go around in circles for a long time without getting anywhere.

Some people hesitate to set goals. One rationale I've heard lately is that it's better to have no goals and be pleasantly surprised when good things happen, than to set goals and be discouraged when you fail to reach them. That's an interesting, but dangerous, approach.

It's idealistic to assume that good things will automatically happen. It's fatalistic to assume that one will fail to reach a goal. Those who set goals achieve them far more often than they fail. They also have more good things happening in their lives.

YOU CAN WANDER ALONG NEVER KNOWING FOR SURE WHERE YOU'RE GOING, OR YOU CAN SET GOALS AND DEVELOP PLANS.

When you're out for a Sunday drive with no destination in mind, you may not need a road map — unless, of course, you become lost and can't find your way home. While Sunday driving may be a relaxing way to spend the afternoon, it's a poor way to spend your life.

Remember, a road map to Miami is no guarantee of a vacation in the sun, but it *will* tell you which way to drive.

29

REVIEWING AND RENEWING

Are the goals we set for ourselves at age 20 adequate for us at age 50?

We all change, thank goodness, so the goals we wrote for ourselves when we were 20 may be inappropriate for the person we've become at 30. We should be ashamed of ourselves if the goals we write at 60 are not vastly different from the goals we wrote at 30! Sometimes the goals we set for ourselves one year are outdated by the next year.

Because we change so much, and the people and events around us change as well, it is important that we review our goals frequently and carefully. The added advantage to this is that we can see the progress we are making as human beings. We can ask ourselves what we were thinking when we wrote previous goals and what has happened to us to cause us to change.

The interesting part of this exercise is that we never totally leave a goal; an old goal or dream is always a part of us, even if it's only a stepping stone.

Review your goals. What new insights will now make an important difference in your life? Where do you go from here?

Each day that we live gives birth to the next. The days string together slowly, until suddenly we have a lifetime behind us.

The fascinating part of getting older is that our goals become clearer and more complex. We can relax a little as we become more determined. We can challenge people more as we love them more. And we can forgive ourselves more often as we constantly push ourselves to grander heights.

> EACH DAY THAT WE LIVE GIVES BIRTH TO THE NEXT.

Each day is new; yet each day is a foundation and a step. You are writing the story of your life every day that you live. How do you want the final chapter to read?

30

REALISTIC GOALS

It is often difficult to identify what is "realistic and obtainable" for you. There is actually a very fine line between the possible and the impossible. On the one hand, you want goals that cause you to stretch yourself to your grandest heights; on the other hand, you don't want to set your goals beyond your reach, or you may doom yourself to failure.

Personally, if I had to err in one direction or another, I'd push myself a little. I say this cautiously, because I know there are many people who have nervous breakdowns by trying to achieve more than they can handle. I've had some close calls myself. But I've also achieved things beyond my wildest dreams and experienced endless joy from knowing I can do it!

There's exhilaration in attacking your fears and pushing the limits you have set for yourself. Once you've learned you have more power and ability than you thought you had, you're anxious to tackle even more, to see what else you can do. It's exciting and fun!

Common wisdom says to set realistic goals. That's basically good advice, but every time I think about realistic goals, a picture flashes through my mind. It's a picture that appeared in a news magazine several years ago. In the picture a woman was grinning from ear to ear. At age 72, she had something amazing to grin about.

A few years earlier she had decided to become a mountain climber. She had never climbed a mountain before. "Mountain climbing ɔt a realistic goal," her friends warned, but ᵓd to do it anyway. She was now in the ᵉ had climbed Mt. Everest!

ᵗˡ her glory, backpack and ɹp toward the clear

blu

> THERE'S EXHILARATION IN ATTACKING YOUR FEARS AND PUSHING THE LIMITS YOU HAVE SET FOR YOURSELF.

What is ᵗᵗ ɑ have to decide for yourself. Whatever you do, don't sell yourself short. When people try to tell you you're not being realistic, remember the 72-year-old mountain climber and go for it!

31

SEVEN STEPS FOR REACHING YOUR GOALS

Everyone knows that setting goals will help you achieve more and adds excitement and meaning to life. But setting a goal is only the beginning. We often fail to follow through, and our goals turn into unfulfilled daydreams. To eliminate that pitfall, here is a systematic, seven-step approach that will help you turn your goals into realities.

1. Decide what you want to achieve. Determine exactly what you want. Be specific. Be sure your goal is measurable, so you can tell when you're making progress. Pick a target date for achieving it. Be sure it is realistically achievable.

2. Ask yourself why it is important for you to achieve this goal. How you will benefit from reaching this goal? Knowing *why* you want something raises your level of motivation. The higher your motivation level, the more likely you are to act on your goal. In addition, highly motivated people are more likely to make any sacrifice necessary to reach their goal.

3. Consider what obstacles, problems, or personal shortcomings might block your progress. List every one you can think of. Some obstacles will be real, others may be only imaginary. You must conquer both.

4. Examine the obstacles one at a time, and think about how you might solve each problem. Ask others to help you brainstorm for solutions.

5. List the people or organizations who could help you achieve your goal. Decide specifically what you will ask them to do.

6. Consider what information you need that you don't have now. Where will you get it? What could you read? Who could you talk to? What seminars could you attend?

WE OFTEN FAIL TO FOLLOW THROUGH AND OUR GOALS TURN INTO UNFULFILLED DAYDREAMS.

7. Write out a detailed action plan for achieving your goal. What are the priorities involved? Which tasks must be done first? When will different actions take place?

Setting a goal is a good step, but it is only the beginning. It takes all seven steps to make sure you actually follow through, and by so doing achieve your goal.

32

HOW TO STAY FOCUSED ON WHAT'S IMPORTANT

Many people tell me they have trouble staying focused on the important issues, because too many other things are happening around them.

What is the really important part of your work? In general, it's those activities that help you reach your goals. The difficulty is that important tasks rarely demand your attention. It's the routine, trivial issues that scream the loudest. The more you give your attention to the trivial demands, the more you risk wandering off track and missing your goal.

I learned a valuable lesson about focus when I worked on a farm one summer. To plow a straight furrow, I learned, you aim at a stationary object on the far side of the field. Keep your eyes on the object, and you can easily drive straight to it. However, if you watch your tractor wheels and the ground immediately ahead, you'll plow a crooked furrow. With a short-range focus you won't realize that you're zig-zagging. A long-range focus creates a straight furrow.

Most jobs are the same: Concentrate on daily trivia and you'll wander off course. Even worse, you won't realize you're wandering away from the goal. To stay on target, you've got to keep your eyes on your long-range goals.

How do you stay focused in the midst of all the daily trivia? Here are four practical ideas.

1. Write out your long-range goals. Make sure you write clear, specific statements about what you want to achieve.

2. Read your long-range goals every day. The more you read them, the more they will help you maintain focus.

> **A LONG-RANGE FOCUS CREATES A STRAIGHT FURROW.**

3. Ask yourself this question continually: "How is what I'm doing right now helping me reach my goals?" Eliminate activities that don't help.

4. Discuss priorities with superiors, subordinates, or team members. Do this regularly, at least once every week.

The choice is yours. Focus on short-range issues, and you'll wind up frustrated and off course. Focus on long-range goals, and you'll stay on track and achieve much more.

35

GUIDING PRINCIPLES CAN HELP YOU SUCCEED

D o you have a philosophy for success? If so, could you reduce your philosophy for success into three simple statements?

Most of us don't even have a philosophy we can identify, and certainly could not explain it in three concise statements. It might be worthwhile to consider developing one.

For example, David Ogilvy, the advertising genius, has three guidelines he claims will inevitably lead to success. 1. Work twice as hard as other people are working. 2. Work at jobs you enjoy doing. 3. Keep working; don't even think about retiring.

GUIDING PRINCIPLES CAN HELP YOU SUCCEED

Sometimes we dismiss guidelines like this as being too simplistic. Consider Ogilvy's guidelines for a minute. They are almost deceptively simple. However, they may be far more useful than many of us would believe.

Just having them or believing them is not the issue. Rather, think about the kind of results you might expect if you acted on them.

Take point one. If your intent is to outwork everyone else, how would you implement it? You would probably be more prepared. You'd start earlier. You'd do more research. You'd try more alternatives.

WORK HARDER THAN ANYONE ELSE, WORK AT SOMETHING YOU ENJOY, AND KEEP WORKING.

Notice how Ogilvy's second point blends with the first one. If you're doing something you really enjoy, you'll naturally become better at it. And when you enjoy your work, it isn't just work anymore.

Then he says never to stop. It's surprising how many of the top people in any field never even think of retiring. They're committed for life, and that makes a big difference.

Three simple guidelines: Work harder than anyone else, work at something you enjoy, and keep working. They may sound simple, but they can make a great model for your own philosophy of success.

34

WHAT TO DO WITH YOUR LIFE

What would you say if a young person asked you what they should do with their life? Dr. Norman Vincent Peale, the famous author and speaker, once told me how he responded to one young man. The conversation went something like this.

"How can I get somewhere with my life?"

"Where do you want to get?"

"I don't know exactly, but definitely somewhere."

"When do you want to get there?"

"I don't know — sometime."

"If you could choose to do anything, what would you like to do best?"

"I don't know. I've never thought about that."

"What are your natural talents? What do you do best now?"

"I don't know."

"Looks to me like you're in a bad fix. You want to get somewhere, but you don't know where, you don't know when, you don't know what you can do best, and you don't know what you'd like to do. How in the world are you going to get anywhere without the answers to those questions?"

These are simple, powerful questions. They are also tough questions to answer. Too many of us just drift through life, assuming that things will take care of themselves. Then we are disappointed when things don't turn out right.

Dr. Peale's advice is sound. It all begins by considering where, when, and what. Where do you want to go? When do you want to get there? What can you do best? Dr. Peale asked the young man to write out his answers. Writing out his answers to those questions helped him tremendously, he said. It has helped many others too.

TOO MANY OF US JUST DRIFT THROUGH LIFE, ASSUMING THAT THINGS WILL TAKE CARE OF THEMSELVES.

Try writing out the answers to these questions yourself. Taking the time to clarify where, when, and what is a good exercise for anyone — young or old.

BEING PROFESSIONAL

Do you see a man skilled in his work?
He will serve before kings; be will not
serve before obscure men.
Proverbs 22:29

35

RIGHT AND WRONG

These days some people seem to have trouble telling right from wrong. Harry Fosdick Emerson developed a formula years ago that might help us today. He called it, "Six Ways to Tell Right from Wrong." He suggested we test our potential actions against these six criteria.

1. *The Common Sense Test.* Are you simply being foolish? How would you judge someone else if they did the same thing?

2. *The Sportsmanship Test.* Are you playing fair? How would you feel if someone else did the same thing to you? If it is not right for everyone, it is probably not right for anyone.

3. *The Best Self Test.* Are you trying to be the best you can be? Will it help you become a better person?

4. *The Publicity Test.* If everyone knew what you were doing, would you still do it? It is surprising how the light of public knowledge changes our perspective and our behavior.

5. *The Most Admired Person Test.* Would the person you most admire do it? If you told that person about it, would you feel proud or ashamed?

6. *The Foresight Test.* What can possibly go wrong? Could you live with those consequences?

These are six tough tests. Any action passing all six tests would probably be a good choice. Emerson provided us with a powerful tool to help determine what is right and what is wrong. If you consistently do what is right, you will gain a strong, positive reputation, both personally and professionally.

This world needs more people who will do what is right just because it's right. By doing this, you will be making the world around you a better place. You will also be setting a good example for others to follow.

THIS WORLD NEEDS MORE PEOPLE WHO WILL DO WHAT IS RIGHT JUST BECAUSE IT'S RIGHT.

36

HOW TO HANDLE CRITICISM

No one really enjoys criticism. We would like to believe we do everything right, even though we know that isn't true. When we do make mistakes, we would rather no one noticed.

People do notice, however, and sometimes they point out our errors. It may even be their job to catch such mistakes and help us to avoid them in the future.

No matter how positive people try to be, criticism hurts. It might take some of the sting out of criticism you receive if you remember these points.

1. Don't be defensive. This only indicates your own insecurity. In addition, emotional outbursts seldom solve anything and usually make matters worse.

2. If you have heard the same criticism more than once, pay close attention. If several people make similar comments, there is probably a valid problem.

3. Consider the source of the criticism. Is the person criticizing you upset about something else? Are they overreacting for some reason?

4. Learn to relax. It may not be easy, but you can learn to relax, even when you are under pressure. Deep, slow breathing helps.

5. Separate your *self* from your *behavior*. Even good people choose wrong actions. Making a mistake does not make you a bad person.

6. Try to learn something. There may be a valuable lesson for you in the criticism. Think it over later when you can be more objective. If the criticism was justified, consider how you might improve.

Although we consider criticism to be negative, it can actually be a positive force in helping us improve ourselves. You may never learn to love it, but you can learn to live with it. The secret is discovering how to respond in a positive way.

> ALTHOUGH WE CONSIDER CRITICISM TO BE NEGATIVE, IT CAN ACTUALLY BE A POSITIVE FORCE IN HELPING US IMPROVE OURSELVES.

37

MOTIVATION BEGINS IN YOUR MIND

An American Indian legend tells about a boy who found an eagle's egg and put it into the nest of a prairie chicken. The eaglet hatched with the brood of chicks and grew up with them.

Thinking he was a prairie chicken all his life, the changeling eagle did what the other prairie chickens did. He scratched in the dirt for seeds and insects to eat. He clucked and cackled. He flew in a brief thrashing of wings and flurry of feathers no more than a few feet off the ground. After all, that's how prairie chickens were supposed to fly.

Years passed, and the changeling eagle grew older. One day he saw a magnificent bird far above him in the cloudless sky. Hanging with graceful majesty on the powerful wind, it soared with scarcely a beat of its golden wings.

"What a beautiful bird!" said the changeling eagle to his neighbor. "What is it?"

"That's an eagle, the chief of birds," his neighbor chicken clucked. "But don't give it a second thought. You could never be like him."

The changeling eagle listened to his neighbor and never gave it a second thought. He died thinking he was a prairie chicken.

What about you? Are you content to scratch in the dirt, or would you rather soar in the sky? If you'd prefer to soar, here are two thoughts which may help.

First, find something to get excited about. Something to look forward to. Something to dream about. Something to devote your life to.

ARE YOU CONTENT TO SCRATCH IN THE DIRT, OR WOULD YOU RATHER SOAR IN THE SKY?

Second, keep telling yourself you can do it. Stay away from cynics and complainers. They're not going anywhere — you are. If you keep telling yourself you can do it, you probably will. Don't let a neighbor chicken tell you not to give your dreams a second thought. Soar with the eagles! Don't die a prairie chicken!

38

TEN RULES FOR DEALING WITH PEOPLE

For many years, Dr. Norman Vincent Peale was a consistent source of excellent ideas for successful living. His books and tapes inspired me to keep working to become a better me. Here are some of the ideas he suggested for getting along better with others. They are sound advice for all of us and worth repeating. Test yourself on each of them to evaluate how you are doing.

1. Learn to remember names. People's names are very important to them. Forgetting a person's name is often taken as a sign you're not very interested in them.

2. Relax and be a comfortable person to be with. Make sure there is no strain in being around you. No one enjoys being around uptight people.

TEN RULES FOR DEALING WITH PEOPLE

3. Learn to be an easy-going person. Take things in stride. Don't let little things bother you.

4. Don't be egotistical or give the impression you know everything. Work at learning from those around you. Learn to respect other people's opinions.

5. Be an interesting person. Stimulate others. Work at becoming the kind of person others want to be around.

6. Smooth out your rough spots. Learn to be gracious, polite, and tactful.

7. Be a peacemaker. Shrug off grievances. Honestly try to correct every misunderstanding you are involved in.

8. Overlook people's faults. Work at choosing to like others until you learn to do it naturally.

9. Boost other people. Encourage them, support them, congratulate them, and tell them why you appreciate them.

WORK AT BECOMING THE KIND OF PERSON OTHERS WANT TO BE AROUND.

10. Develop spiritual depth so you have something to pass on to others. Learn to share this strength with people you meet.

Have you mastered all these points? I must confess, I haven't. There is still much I can improve. In his 90s, Dr. Peale even admitted there were still things he needed to work on. The important point is that he was still working on them. Are you?

39

ARE BUSINESS AND ETHICS COMPATIBLE?

Many people consider the term, "business ethics," a contradiction. I heard someone say, "Just try being ethical in this field. The competition will eat you alive." The implication is that caring, ethical behavior puts you at a serious disadvantage. Everyone seems to believe that nice guys finish last.

Well, almost everyone. Tad Tuleja, author of the book, *Beyond the Bottom Line*, maintains that companies which do right ethically also tend to do well financially.

How do you define an "ethical company"? Tuleja suggests measuring the ethics of a company the same way you would measure any ethical behavior. He says the best measure is how closely they adhere to the Golden Rule, that if you treat other people the way you would like to be treated yourself, you end up making a better profit.

Tuleja's research indicates that ethical firms have a genuine concern for their employees, their customers, and society in general. He points out that people work better when they believe their company cares about them. This leads to better products and services, greater sales, and more profits.

Is there any evidence to support this belief? Tuleja says yes. For example, he points to a study done by the Center for Economic Revitalization. They selected several firms that met certain ethical criteria, like maintaining responsible employee relations and supporting public service programs. Then they compared the performance of these companies to the firms that make up the Dow Jones Average. Over a ten-year period, the Dow Jones Average rose 55 percent, while the average increase for the ethical firms was 240 percent.

IF YOU TREAT OTHER PEOPLE THE WAY YOU WOULD LIKE TO BE TREATED YOURSELF, YOU END UP MAKING A BETTER PROFIT.

Good ethics makes good business sense. Now that is good news! It appears they have discovered that nice guys actually finish *first*.

40

CAUSE & EFFECT LAWS OF LIFE

S cience teaches us that for every action there is an equal and opposite reaction. While we know this applies to the physical realm, we often forget that it also applies to the emotional realm. I was reminded of this recently when I found a copy of the poem entitled, *The Laws of Life*. It contains 15 truths about cause-effect relationships, each of them valuable for molding a better me — and a better you.

The more generous we are, the more joyous we become.

The more enthusiastic we are, the more valuable we become.

The more interested we are, the more alive we become.

The more caring we are, the more radiant we become.

The more serving we are, the more prosperous we become.

The more outgoing we are, the more helpful we become.

The more persistent we are, the more successful we become.

The more grateful we are, the more godly we become.

The more forgiving we are, the freer we become.

The more prayerful we are, the more blessed we become.

The more curious we are, the more creative we become.

The more trusting we are, the wiser we become.

The more patient we are, the more responsive we become.

The more considerate we are, the more peaceful we become.

The more cheerful we are, the more attractive we become.

This great poem reminds us that we're each in charge of ourselves and points out specific ways we can become a better person — if we want to. It also tells us what the rewards will be for living in this way. If we plant the seeds, we will reap the harvest.

SCIENCE TEACHES US THAT FOR EVERY ACTION THERE IS AN EQUAL AND OPPOSITE REACTION.

41

BIBLICAL PROVERBS

D o you study the wisdom expressed by the book of Proverbs in the Bible?

I love proverbs of all kinds. I've been collecting them for years, but I especially love the book of Proverbs in the Bible. They are not only wise sayings, but they are wise sayings inspired by God. For me, that makes them the very best proverbs of all.

The other day, I was reviewing several of the work-related proverbs from the *New International Version* of the Bible. Perhaps they will help you as much as they helped me.

Here's a good one from Proverbs 12:11: "He who works his land will have abundant food, but he who chases fantasies lacks judgment." An almost identical version is found in Proverbs 28:19:

"He who works his land will have abundant food, but the one who chases fantasies will have his fill of poverty." Someone once told me that when God goes to the trouble of repeating something, we ought to pay very close attention to it.

A similar thought is found in Proverbs 14:23. "All hard work brings a profit, but mere talk leads only to poverty." All talk and no action. Maybe this kind of chatter is another form of chasing fantasies.

Reading Proverbs is good; reading them and applying them to your life is better. An acquaintance of mine has been talking for years about how he is going to really make it big one of these days. His big break is bound to come any time now. Problem is, he isn't doing much in the meantime, except talking about what he is going to do — someday. Maybe he will, but those of us who have been listening to him for years aren't so sure.

READING PROVERBS IS GOOD; READING THEM AND APPLYING THEM TO YOUR LIFE IS BETTER.

Spend some time studying the book of Proverbs in the Bible. It can provide important insight which will start you, and keep you, moving in the right direction.

42

THE SERENITY PRAYER

I've always enjoyed the serenity prayer. Are you familiar with it?

"God, grant me the serenity to accept the things I cannot change; the courage to change the things I can; and the wisdom to know the difference."

Serenity, courage, and wisdom are three things we can all use these days.

Serenity is a wonderful way to live — calm, quiet, tranquil, peaceful. Serene people don't get upset when things don't go their way. They are more relaxed, and they are more relaxing to be with. They are more likely to promote peaceful relationships, and are not eager to stir up strife.

Some might say that serene people are wimps. The blustering, brawling, macho male image is receiving increased attention once again. Some of us seem to admire destroyers more than peacemakers. However, serene doesn't mean sissy; just the opposite. It requires tremendous inner strength to maintain serenity.

Next, there is courage. The courage to change the things we can. Too many of us don't try to change anything. We play the "Somebody-Oughta-Do-Something-About-That" game. There are dozens of opportunities for each of us to change something, thereby making an improvement in our life or someone else's. Yet, too often we choose to stand by and complain rather than go to work to change something.

TOO MANY OF US DON'T TRY TO CHANGE ANYTHING.

I saw a sign the other day that has been on my mind ever since. It said, "One man with courage makes a majority." Hmmm. Am I really a man of courage? Are you?

Finally, wisdom. Wisdom is knowledge, insight, judgment, good sense, and prudence. It often takes a great deal of wisdom to decide whether something should be accepted or changed, whether you can do something about it, or you can't.

Serenity, courage, and wisdom — three things we could all use more of. May God grant them to us as we earnestly seek them.

43

TAKE TIME TO HELP SOMEONE ELSE

I f you'd really like to feel good about yourself, try helping someone else.

Americans love to give. They give their money and they give their time. Some of the happiest people I know are those who are so busy giving to others, they never have time to fret about their own problems.

Most of the giving we do is never publicized. We don't give for publicity; we give because we believe in helping others. But every now and then, someone's gift is noticed, and it inspires others.

Eugene Lang is a good example. Discouraged by the high percentage of students who drop out and never finish high school, he did a most unusual thing. While talking to sixth graders at the school he once attended, he promised every one of them if they would graduate from high school and get accepted to college, he would personally guarantee their college tuition.

Inspired by this story, a group of Boston businessmen got together and developed a plan of their own. They not only promised to help the Boston inner-city students through college, but promised each of them a job when they graduated.

I admire anyone who takes the time to help others, whether they're doing big things or little things. I'm thrilled to read about people like Eugene Lang, but I'm just as excited about people all over this country who are doing thousands of little things we'll never hear about.

Once when I was feeling rather sorry for myself, my grandmother suggested that helping someone else would be a good antidote for what ailed me. She was right, and I heartily recommend it. You haven't lived until you've experienced the warm glow of unselfishly helping someone else, especially someone who can never return the favor.

> SOME OF THE HAPPIEST PEOPLE I KNOW ARE THOSE WHO ARE SO BUSY GIVING TO OTHERS THAT THEY NEVER HAVE TIME TO FRET ABOUT THEIR OWN PROBLEMS.

While you may not be in a position to do what Eugene Lang or the Boston businessmen did, you can help someone. Pick up groceries for an elderly neighbor, teach a new coworker the ropes, give a lonely-looking stranger a smile. Look around you, every person you see has a need of some kind. If you can only help one, you've made a difference.

44

ARE SUPER-SUCCESSFUL PEOPLE DIFFERENT?

According to *Execu-Time* newsletter, it isn't just fame and fortune that separates the super-successful from the rest of us. They think, work, and live differently. Here are 12 of the traits that *Execu-Time* says super-successful people are likely to exhibit.

1. They like their vocation. If they could start their careers over again, they would choose the same or a very similar road.

2. They prefer work to hobbies. In their spare time, they tend to enjoy mental activities, like reading, over sports or other physical activities.

3. They are socially outgoing. They don't bemoan the fact that

they don't know anyone at a party. Instead, they circulate and introduce themselves.

4. They are optimistic, but practical. They have a positive, "can-do" attitude. However, they will take a proven route rather than search for a pie-in-the-sky answer.

5. They still believe in Horatio Alger. They believe the dream of rags-to-riches is still possible.

6. They are very healthy and seldom require sick days.

7. They were not model children. They were usually leaders as youngsters, but not angels. They were often mischievous.

8. They think they are lucky and that they will continue to be lucky.

9. They concentrate well, enabling them to focus on "the business at hand."

> IT ISN'T JUST FAME AND FORTUNE THAT SEPARATES THE SUPER-SUCCESSFUL FROM THE REST OF US.

10. They draw on intuition as well as rational information when making decisions.

11. They know people of all social levels and have extremely large numbers of acquaintances, which means they have many useful contacts.

12. They don't get bogged down by details, but strive to see the big picture.

Having all these characteristics is not guaranteed to make you super-successful, but it's a great place to start.

45

A GOOD ATTITUDE MAKES A GOOD JOB

Everyone wants a good job. Exactly what is it, though, that makes one job good and another job not so good? Comedian Sam Levenson once said, "When my immigrant father came here from the old country, he found out three things: that the streets were not paved with gold; that most of the streets were not even paved; and that he had to help pave them."

We would all like to have big, glamorous, important jobs. What we find when we get one, however, is that it is full of mundane details and isn't so glamorous after all. It can even get downright boring some days. We have to do many things we really don't want to do. We forget that small, dull, routine jobs can also be important.

A GOOD ATTITUDE MAKES A GOOD JOB

Many years ago when I was complaining about being stuck in a "bad" job, I received some good advice. A friend suggested that if I couldn't find a job I liked, I should concentrate on what I liked in the job I had. He went on to say that my attitude flavored the way I looked at my job.

Attitude is important. A good attitude can make a good job. A poor attitude can turn even the best job sour. In almost any job there is usually an element of excitement involved; whether or not we find that excitement depends on our attitude.

Here are two thoughts to help you maintain a "good job" attitude. First, think about who or what benefits by what you do. Even if you're only a small part in a major operation, remember that each and every link is important — that makes you important.

A GOOD ATTITUDE CAN MAKE A GOOD JOB.

Second, think about how you could improve what you're doing. Striving to meet a challenge can add excitement to any job.

Your job can be wonderful or miserable. Believe it or not, the difference is up to you. It's all in your attitude.

46

POSITIVE WORDS CREATE POSITIVE PEOPLE

What you say to yourself about yourself makes all the difference in the world. You tend to act out your conversations with yourself and become what you've told yourself. For example, if you tell yourself often enough that you are not creative, you probably won't be. On the other hand, if you tell yourself you are creative, you will generate many innovative ideas.

Whether you think of yourself as a winner or a loser helps determine what actually happens to you. You tend to act in ways that are consistent with what you believe about yourself. What you believe is what you keep repeating to yourself. In other words, what you say to yourself, over and over, helps make you the person you are. Changing what you say to yourself can help you become a better person.

To change yourself, try using positive affirmations. Positive affirmations are simply positive statements about the kind of person you wish to be. Here are two examples of positive affirmation that you might consider. "I choose my attitude in every circumstance. It isn't what happens that is most important, but how I respond to what happens."

Here is another good one. "I am responsible for my feelings. No one else can make me feel one way or another. That is up to me."

CHANGING WHAT YOU SAY TO YOURSELF CAN HELP YOU BECOME A BETTER PERSON.

The idea behind using affirmation is simple. You continually read or repeat the message until it penetrates your subconscious. It is now a permanent part of you. When you concentrate on positive statements in this way, you are literally shaping yourself into a positive person.

Test this for yourself. Write down several positive affirmations on index cards. Read them several times a day for two weeks. Repeat them out loud. You'll soon discover for yourself just how powerful positive affirmation can be.

47

WHEN YOU FEEL LIKE QUITTING

L ife can be tough. Sooner or later we all get discouraged and feel like quitting. It can be difficult to keep going when nothing seems to be working out right.

Several years ago, United Technologies Corporation ran one of their famous advertisements in *The Wall Street Journal*. Reading it always helps me overcome discouragement. This is what it said:

"Is that what you want to do? Quit? Anybody can do that. Takes no talent. Takes no guts. It's exactly what your adversaries hope you will do. Get your facts straight. Know what you're talking about. And keep going. In the 1948 Presidential election, the nation's leading political reporters all predicted Harry Truman would lose. He won. Winston

Churchill said, 'Never give in. Never. Never.' Sir Winston stuck his chin out and wouldn't quit. Try sticking out your chin. Don't give up. Ever."

Abraham Lincoln is probably our best loved and most quoted President. He faced many defeats before he was elected President of the United States. In 1832 he lost his job and was defeated for the legislature. In 1833 he failed in business. In 1836 he had a nervous breakdown. In 1838 he was defeated for Speaker. In 1843 he was defeated for Congress. In 1848 he lost the nomination bid for Congress. In 1854 he was defeated for the Senate. In 1856 he lost the nomination for Vice President. In 1858 he was again defeated for the Senate. Then finally, in 1860 he was elected President.

QUITTERS NEVER MAKE IT TO THE WINNER'S CIRCLE.

There were many times when Lincoln could have given up. No one would have blamed him if he had. In fact, many advised him to. However, if he had given up he would never have been elected President.

Don't quit! Quitters never make it to the winner's circle. Hang in there. Others have made it, and so can you!

48

MASTER THE DETAILS

This may strike you as silly, but have you ever been bitten by an elephant? Probably not. I have never known anyone who was bitten by an elephant. But what about a mosquito? Everyone has been bitten by a mosquito. My friend, Joel Weldon, once posed those questions to an audience. He said our responses could teach us a lesson. It is not the big things that get us; it is the little things.

This is absolutely true, but many of us pay more attention to the big things than to the small details. Golfers have a quaint expression: "Drive for show, putt for dough." The big, powerful shot off the tee is not the key to winning the game. Long drives impress the crowd, but golfers who have mastered putting are more often the winners. You will still hear golfers talking more about how far they can drive the ball than how well they can putt, and most golfers practice driving more than they practice putting.

Mastering the details is also known as a winning football strategy. The New England Patriots football team can credit mastering mundane details as a key reason for their 1985 championship season. They practiced recovering fumbled footballs. Not a very glamorous play, but certainly a critical one. The result was the best fumble recovery record in a league where the team who recovers the most fumbles is often the team that wins. Yet, in the beginning many of the Patriot players thought all that practice was dumb.

> IT IS NOT THE BIG THINGS THAT GET US; IT IS THE LITTLE THINGS.

When you feel tempted to rush over the details, stop and think a minute. Mastering the details may be boring and dull, but if you don't you are not likely to stand in the winner's circle. Dr. Kenneth McFarlane, one of the all-time great sales trainers, used to say, "Spectacular performance must always be preceded by unspectacular preparation."

Forget about the elephants and pay more attention to the mosquitoes!

49

GET TO THE POINT QUICKLY

Some people waste a lot of time getting to the point. They wander all over the subject instead of cutting right to the heart of the matter, making the rest of us bored, impatient, and frustrated. When that happens, communication ceases.

Getting to the point is a very valuable skill in business. You will seldom hear criticism for being able to make your point quickly. Most complaints are about people who take forever to tell you what they have to say.

Milo Frank's book, *How To Get Your Point Across In 30 Seconds Or Less*, offers sound advice. The basis, according to Mr. Frank, is to begin by having a single, clear-cut objective. Exactly what do you want? Next, carefully consider the person you are talking to. Then use a well formulated approach geared to communicate to that person. In other words, carefully think about what you are after, who you are talking to, and how best to say what you have to say.

Mr. Frank also recommends using a hook. A hook is a statement or object specifically used to capture someone's attention. In a newspaper, for example, the headline is a hook. The purpose of the headline is to hook you into reading the article.

Use your hook at the beginning of your communication to gain the listener's attention. Hooks can be dramatic or humorous, statements or questions, anecdotes or personal experiences. However, be sure that the hook you choose relates to your objective.

YOU WILL SELDOM HEAR CRITICISM FOR BEING ABLE TO MAKE YOUR POINT QUICKLY.

The average adult attention span is declining. It is more important than ever to get to the point quickly. To do so, just follow Milo Frank's four simple guidelines. Consider what you want, who you are talking to, the best way to say what you have to say, and how to hook their attention.

50

WHAT TO DO WHEN YOU'RE BORED WITH YOUR JOB

Sooner or later almost everyone gets bored with their job. Maybe it's just a case of "spring fever." It could be the psychological let-down following the completion of a major project. Or maybe your job has simply become mindlessly routine.

Those people who have more mundane jobs often dream about having exciting, glamorous jobs. "Give me a job like that," they say, "and I'll never be bored." But people who have glamorous jobs wrestle with bouts of boredom just like the rest of us. No matter what you're doing, if you've been doing it long enough, it can seem as routine and dull as typing address labels all day long.

WHAT TO DO WHEN YOU'RE BORED WITH YOUR JOB

Chronic or severe boredom may signal burnout. If that's the case, you should seek help from a professional counselor. Usually, however, boredom is temporary, and you can easily do something about it.

Job-stress experts suggest taking a few days off if you can. Relax and do something really different. If your job is primarily intellectual, then do something physical, and vice-versa. Maintaining good mental health requires regular breaks from your normal routine.

You might also analyze your job. What parts do you like and what parts do you dislike? If you find you dislike more than you like, that could contribute to your boredom. Think of ways you could replace the parts you dislike with something you would like better. Is there something different you could do that would make an even greater contribution to your company? Could you do a routine task in a different way? Analyzing these things can help you to refocus your job; maybe even create a better one.

MAINTAINING GOOD MENTAL HEALTH REQUIRES REGULAR BREAKS FROM YOUR NORMAL ROUTINE.

Sometimes you can't change your job, but you can find something challenging to do in your leisure hours. Start a new hobby, take up a new sport, work on someone's political campaign. Boredom at home piled on top of boredom at work is a terrible burden. So experiment! Find something you enjoy doing and do it!

51

DON'T BE A 95-PERCENTER

D o you sometimes fizzle out right at the end of a project? It happens to me every now and then, even though I'm supposed to know better.

I once agreed to deliver a manuscript to a publisher by the 15th. It actually got there on the 25th. It was absolutely my fault. The manuscript was actually finished on the 9th, but I didn't write the cover letter and put it in the mail right then. I should have, but I was tired. The day was over and besides, I had plenty of time to do it later. Then, something else came up and I forgot all about it until the publisher called me on the 16th.

Many of us are like this. We're "95-percenters." We go full force on something and then run out of steam for one reason or another.

It usually happens when the end is in sight, when we know we can easily finish. The results are poor performance, criticism, and missed deadlines. We also feel guilty and frustrated.

In the 1980 Summer Olympic Games, two runners were ahead of everyone else. The one in front looked like a sure winner. With only a few yards to go, he turned his head to smile at the crowd. In that instant the second place runner went ahead. The front runner relaxed too soon, and it cost him the gold medal.

"THE JOB ISN'T FINISHED UNTIL THE TOOLS ARE PUT AWAY."

When I was a teenager, I once worked for a company assembling farm machinery. I can still remember my employer saying, "The job isn't finished until the tools are put away." I grumbled about it at the time, but today I know he was right. Every time I slow down before the end I usually pay a penalty of some sort.

For best results, don't let up. Keep going until you're finished. 95 percent isn't good enough.

52

HOW TO BOOST YOUR CONFIDENCE LEVEL

Many of us are a little lacking in self-confidence. Much of what we do and say tells others our confidence level is low. We would like to change, but we aren't sure how.

Change *is* achievable. Here are ten good tips from the experts which can help you improve your confidence level.

1. Don't put yourself down. The more you talk about your perceived inadequacies, the more you become bound by them.

2. Don't apologize for being you. You are someone special. You are unique. You have strengths as well as weaknesses.

3. Be decisive. Don't say maybe; say yes or no. Make up your mind and stick to your decision.

HOW TO BOOST YOUR CONFIDENCE LEVEL

4. Don't say, "I can't." Instead say, "Maybe I can; I'll try it."

5. Don't procrastinate. Make a move forward. Even a small move starts your energy flowing and leads to bigger moves.

6. Think about your positive points. Write a list of them and read it often.

7. Volunteer more often. Whenever you have the chance, take on new responsibilities that will challenge you. Start with small things and work up to bigger things.

8. Dream a little. Picture yourself as you really want to be. See yourself doing well, and think about how you would be feeling.

9. Set goals. Begin turning your dreams into reality. List the necessary steps to reach your goals. Take the first step.

10. Play the part. Act as if you are as confident as you want to be. Dress well. Look people in the eye. Speak distinctly. Shake hands firmly. Walk, talk, and act confidently, and you will soon feel more confident too.

> **WALK, TALK AND ACT CONFIDENTLY, AND YOU WILL SOON FEEL MORE CONFIDENT, TOO.**

Ten good tips for improving your confidence level. Why not try them and see how well they work? It won't take long before you notice a positive change in your life.

53

WHAT TO DO WHEN THINGS GO WRONG

When things go wrong, how do you go about making them right? The answer to that question is the theme of a book by Dr. Paul Faulkner. His main point is that things will go wrong, no matter what. That's just the way life is. And when they do, we will have some kind of response. Unfortunately, he says, our response is usually a negative one.

What Dr. Faulkner points out, however, is that we would be a lot better off if we would choose a positive response when things go wrong. His book describes several possibilities. For instance, instead of crying and complaining about our circumstances, we could choose to treat them as a learning experience. Consider the positive lessons we can learn.

Another of Dr. Faulkner's suggestions is to act as if nothing is wrong. When things go wrong, our negative responses trigger negative attitudes, which reinforce more negative responses, and so forth. This downward spiral can be averted by changing our actions, which will then change our attitude, therefore making it easier to take more beneficial action.

For instance, suppose someone makes a comment that hurts your feelings. The tendency is to strike back, which could escalate into hostility. However, you could choose to act as if your feelings were not hurt. It is not easy, but it does work.

WE WOULD BE A LOT BETTER OFF IF WE WOULD CHOOSE A POSITIVE RESPONSE WHEN THINGS GO WRONG.

Because much of what goes wrong involves personal relationships, Dr. Faulkner also suggests that when things go wrong we should take the initiative to make things right. Don't wait for the other person; make the first move yourself, even if it is not your fault.

Look on the bright side, behave as if things are really okay, and act first to patch things up in relationships. These are three ways to help make things right when they go wrong.

54

BEING POLITE COSTS NOTHING

Have you ever thought about how much nicer the world would be if you were always polite to the people you meet? Being polite costs nothing, but it pays great dividends.

I made a big mistake the other day. I had flown to San Jose, California, and got in a taxi to go to the hotel. I told the taxi driver to go to the Sainte Claire Hotel. He thought I was saying Santa Clara, a neighboring city, and kept asking where I wanted to go in Santa Clara. What we had was a simple misunderstanding that I should have been able to easily correct.

However, I was needlessly rude. After two or three attempts to tell him the hotel name, and obviously not getting through, I said if he did not know the city to stop and let me get another taxi. I wished I had not said it, even as the words were coming out of my mouth.

The taxi driver immediately became defensive and said something negative in return. I had alienated the man for no good reason, and I could not figure out why I'd done it.

By that time the taxi driver was angry with me, and I was angry with me too. Neither of us was enjoying the trip, and the driver still didn't know where I wanted to go. He probably didn't even care.

Finally, I found the reservation receipt from the hotel and handed it to him. He read the name and address and handed it back to me, muttering something I couldn't hear. Probably a less than flattering comment.

BEING POLITE COSTS NOTHING, BUT IT PAYS GREAT DIVIDENDS.

We rode along in silence. He was no doubt upset, and I was feeling childish and guilty. I kept thinking about how much better it would have been if I had simply given him the reservation slip earlier, with some kind of positive comment. We could have had a pleasant trip together instead of the miserable ride we both endured.

55

HANDLING VERBAL CURVES

W hat do you do when someone tosses you a verbal curve? We have all been asked those tricky questions like, "Have you stopped beating your wife?" If you're not careful, your response can leave you boxed in or dreadfully embarrassed. The key is to stop a moment and think before you answer. You don't want to be too hasty in responding to those kinds of questions.

Joan Detz, writing in *Success Magazine*, advised that you remember you have three basic rights when confronted with a tricky question: 1) You have the right to be treated fairly; 2) You have the right to stay in control of yourself; and 3) You have the right to get your message across — correctly.

Too often we snap the bait when asked a tricky question. When we do, we are playing the questioner's game, and we seldom come out looking good. As I have listened to people who cleverly side-step the traps, I have learned a small clue. They frequently do not answer the question asked.

A reporter recently asked our mayor if he favored Plan A or Plan B for developing our city. No matter which one he picked, he would have had problems. Instead, he picked neither and said, "The advantages and disadvantages of both Plan A and Plan B are being studied now. Of course, these are only two of the possible courses we could pursue."

Whatever you do, Miss Detz cautions against saying, "No comment." I agree with her. Whenever we hear someone say, "No comment," we automatically assume they are guilty, trying to hide something, or have some devious reason for being evasive.

REMEMBER YOUR RIGHTS — FAIRNESS, SELF-CONTROL, AND COMMUNICATION.

The next time someone tosses you a verbal curve, stop and think before you respond. Don't try to be cute, just be cautious. Don't let yourself be forced into a position you don't want to be in. Remember your rights — fairness, self-control, and communication.

56

HOW TO KEEP GROWING POSITIVELY

D o you periodically take time to assess your personal progress?

I am not talking about money or promotions. Rather, it is the person you are or the one you are becoming that is the focus of a self-evaluation. At least once a year, it is a good idea to pause and take a thorough look at yourself. Here are several questions that can help get your self-assessment started.

1. How much have I learned about the people I live with and work with? Do I know and understand them better than I did a year ago?

2. How many new people have I gotten to know this year?

3. Have I alienated anyone this year? Was it avoidable? What have I done to restore the relationship?

4. Is my personal reputation as good or better than it was a year ago? What events have affected my reputation most?

5. Have I faced any personal challenges during the past year? If so, how did I handle them? What did I learn in the process?

6. Have I learned any new skills in the past year? How have my interpersonal skills, my analytical skills, or my judgment improved?

7. Has my self-discipline improved? Am I able to control myself better?

AT LEAST ONCE A YEAR, IT IS A GOOD IDEA TO PAUSE AND TAKE A THOROUGH LOOK AT YOURSELF.

If you have never checked yourself in this manner before, it may be a bit tough the first time. Don't worry about considering every little thing that has happened to you in the past year. Just step back and take an arm's length look at yourself. Look at the high points and low points. Try to be as honest and objective as you can. You might even want to ask your spouse or a good friend to help you.

Why go to the trouble of checking up on yourself? Because regularly assessing yourself can be an excellent way to guarantee consistent personal growth.

57

TWO RULES FOR GOOD RELATIONSHIPS

D id you ever speak without thinking, and then wish you could take back what you said? I sure have — too many times. I did it again just yesterday.

I was hassled, rushed, and upset, and I spoke to someone rudely. It wasn't right and it certainly wasn't pleasant. I was wrong and I knew it.

However, being rude was only my first mistake. My second mistake was failing to apologize for my unkind remark. Instead, I just sat there in silence, wondering when I was going to grow up.

Most of the time I am quick to admit my errors and apologize for inappropriate behavior. But every now and then, my old stubborn streak reasserts itself. Rather than apologize and try to restore a relationship, I choose to withdraw behind a wall of stony silence.

The problem is, this stony silence never produces a positive effect; it usually makes matters worse. I try to justify my poor behavior and look for ways to prove it was really the other person's fault. This, of course, widens the gap and makes it increasingly difficult to heal the wounded relationship.

If only I could have taken back those ill-chosen words! But I couldn't, and soon it escalated to a matter of pride. To apologize at that point would have been a sign of weakness, so I decided to tough it out.

What started as a small error mushroomed into a major issue. I was boxed in and didn't know where to turn. The only way out was to apologize, but after a period of time it seemed almost impossible. What would have been relatively easy to do earlier, was infinitely harder to do later. The alternative meant cutting off the relationship, and I didn't want to do that either.

WHAT STARTED AS A SMALL ERROR HAD NOW MUSHROOMED INTO A MAJOR ISSUE.

From painful experiences like this I am slowly learning two immutable rules. The more I use them, the better they work. Rule 1: Think before you speak. Rule 2: When you forget or ignore Rule 1, apologize quickly.

58

ARE YOU EXPERIENCING ANY OF THESE SYMPTOMS?

How can you tell when you are headed for trouble? What are the symptoms to watch for?

A colleague sent me a paper entitled, "Profile of an Executive in Trouble." Here is what it said.

1. He fights change. He struggles to maintain the status quo. He opposes the new and strives to repeat the past.

2. He becomes defensive. He doesn't like being questioned or challenged. He guards against attack and never sticks his neck out.

3. He is inflexible. He won't budge from his position. He won't bend or compromise.

ARE YOU EXPERIENCING ANY OF THESE SYMPTOMS?

4. He has no team spirit. He wants to do it all himself. He doesn't even want suggestions.

5. He has personal problems. He drinks too much and has family troubles.

6. He is fat and lazy. He feels he has arrived and is entitled to have the company carry him from now on.

7. He won't take a risk. New products, new systems, or competition of any kind is too hazardous.

8. He lacks imagination. He can't, or won't, think creatively. He won't stretch his mind or broaden his horizons.

9. He is disorganized. He does unimportant work first. He jumps around from task to task. He is a poor planner.

10. He has temper tantrums. He rants and raves and hollers at people. He intimidates others. He can't control his emotions.

THESE SYMPTOMS CAN SPELL TROUBLE FOR ANY OF US, NOT JUST EXECUTIVES.

11. He passes the buck. He won't accept responsibility. He is always blaming others.

12. He lacks understanding of others. He doesn't listen well. He isn't sympathetic, kind, or helpful.

These symptoms can spell trouble for any of us, not just executives.

How do you rate? Why not ask some of the people around you what they think?

59

DO YOU FEEL SECURE?

D o you feel safe and secure in your company?

Dr. Tom Brown, a columnist for *Industry Week* magazine, once wrote about management illusions. He said, "Many managers are myopic. They allow themselves the ultimate illusion that they will always be successful. The warm blanket of corporate security has become just a bit too snug, too comfy. The immense quantity of steel and concrete in the corporate headquarters building looks too solid and secure to ever fade away. The annual revenue in millions or billions sounds just too terrific. Hundreds of people sprinting to and fro in the factories dazzle one into feeling an army is on the march with a firm mandate to exist and grow."

DO YOU FEEL SECURE?

I recently conducted a series of seminars for a firm in Texas. They used to have five large divisions; now they have four. The fifth division all but disappeared, falling from 805 employees last year to six people today. What had looked like their strongest area was the first to fall.

Continual success is never guaranteed. The moment you begin to rest on your laurels is the time to start worrying. Just when you think you have got it made, it can easily fall apart.

WHAT WILL IT TAKE TO BE SUCCESSFUL IN THE FUTURE?

Comfort is a deadly trap. History teaches us that soft living leads to decline. Struggle produces progress. Satisfied people don't push for change or growth.

Even recent history should teach us a valuable lesson. Who could have predicted that the wealthy Hunt brothers in Texas would be in bankruptcy? The entire country was shocked by the failure of national institutions like Chrysler Motors, Penn Central Railroad, and Continental Illinois Bank.

When things seem too good to be true, perhaps they are. That is when it is time to ask questions. What will it take to be successful in the future? Where is the company most vulnerable? What trends and developments will pose major threats to survival?

Just remember the old proverb, "What goes up, must come down." No one gets only ups in life.

60

JUMPING TO CONCLUSIONS

Do you jump to conclusions? Do you pass off guesses and opinions as if they were statement of fact? Do you confuse inferential statements with factual statements?

Ready to plead guilty? Then you're both normal and honest. We all get confused about what is fact and what isn't. Dr. S. I. Hayakawa, the renowned semanticist, noted, "The question is not whether or not we make inferences, the question is whether or not we are aware of the inferences we make."

Dr. Hayakawa went on to say, "People talk a great deal of nonsense today because society requires them to have opinions on everything. They talk whether they know anything about the subject or not; and after a while, they begin to believe what they say."

Throughout the ages, wise men have warned against this deception. Plato said, "We become what we contemplate." Ralph Waldo Emerson said, "The office of the scholar is to cheer, to raise, to guide men by showing them facts amidst appearances." Bertrand Russell pointed out, "It is characteristic of the advance of science that less and less is found to be fact, and more and more is found to be inference."

Asking questions can be a useful tactic to enhance our wisdom. Ask, "How do you know?" Perhaps even better, ask yourself, "How do I know?" It will help you stop and think about where you got your facts and whether they are facts at all. That, in turn, will help assure you that you know what you're talking about.

One aspect of wisdom is knowing the difference between statements of fact and statements of inference. When we know the difference, we'll stop jumping to conclusions or presuming to have knowledge we simply do not possess.

ONE ASPECT OF WISDOM IS KNOWING THE DIFFERENCE BETWEEN STATEMENTS OF FACT AND STATEMENTS OF INFERENCE.

61

WHAT GOES IN IS WHAT COMES OUT

H ave you ever thought about how much your mind is like a computer?

When my daughters were young, they loved to play children's music tapes. One song had a verse that went,

"Input, output, that is what it's all about.

Input, output, what goes in is what comes out.

Input, output, your mind is a computer whose,

Input, output, daily you must choose."

That verse contains a powerful message for all of us.

Computer people talk about the garbage-can model: garbage in, garbage out. You have to be very careful when you program a computer. Even the smallest error will produce flawed results. In other words, the results produced by the computer will be no better than the quality of the programming.

People are the same way. What goes in is what comes out. Garbage in, garbage out, just like a computer. Psychologists say we tend to become what we think about most. Proverbs 23:7 in the Bible said the same thing thousands of years ago.

You and I must be careful about what goes into our minds. If we want great ideas to come out, we must put great ideas in. If we want positive attitudes to come out, we must put positive information in. If we want thoughtful, courteous, edifying words and deeds to come out,

GARBAGE IN, GARBAGE OUT.

we must put the right kind of building materials in. An old proverb summarizes this well: You can't make a silk purse from a sow's ear.

What kinds of books do you read? Which magazines do you look at most? What music do you listen to? What do you hear on the radio? Which TV shows and movies do you watch? Do all of these things help you become a better person? Don't just defend your habits, think about them seriously.

Remember, your mind is like a computer, only more complex and advanced. Input, output. What goes in is what comes out. Control your input, and your output will take care of itself.

62

TACKLING GREAT CHALLENGES

A re you sometimes timid about tackling great challenges? Are you little afraid of taking on big jobs?

One of my friends wanted to teach in a nursing school. She had been a nurse for several years, but she did not have a college degree. "No problem," I said, "just go back to school."

Well, it wasn't only a bachelor's degree she needed, but also a master's degree. This would require four or five years of schooling, and she had two children at home. Plus, she hadn't been to school for a long time, and she didn't even know where to begin. Like many of us, she was looking at everything all at once, seeing only the big picture, and feeling quite overwhelmed. As a result, she was crushed by the enormity of the challenge.

An old Chinese proverb says, "A journey of a thousand miles begins with a single step." Focusing on the entire journey can be exhausting and will often keep us from trying. Concentrating on just the first step, however, is not overwhelming at all. Anyone can take the first step, once they know what it is. This principle is a key for all achievement. Any great challenge can be broken down into bite-size tasks that can be tackled one at a time.

We helped our friend overcome her challenge by breaking it into smaller and smaller steps. Whenever she felt overwhelmed, we helped her shift her focus off the big picture and onto the next small step. She finished her bachelor's degree, received her master's degree with honors, and is now teaching in a nursing school. She met her great challenge.

> "A JOURNEY OF A THOUSAND MILES BEGINS WITH A SINGLE STEP."

This is an amazing principle you can use whenever you're facing a great challenge. Just break it down into bite-size pieces. Robert Schuller said it this way: "Yard by yard, life is hard; but inch by inch, life's a cinch." Break your challenge into small steps and always focus on the next step. You will be surprised at how much you can accomplish — one step at a time.

63

ACTIONS VERSUS FEELINGS

D o you sometimes feel "down in the dumps," "kind of miserable," or "blue"?

Sooner or later we all get down. Sometimes we just don't feel like being cheerful, so we act like we feel — depressed. That might not be so bad if we could hibernate until we're feeling better, but what if we can't? What if we have to go to work anyway, attend meetings, or call on customers? Acting gloomy and depressed dampens the spirit of everyone else we contact, and it certainly won't get good results.

The best thing to do is fake it. Don't act like you feel; act the way you want to feel. If you feel depressed, act as if you're happy. If you feel like sighing, laugh instead. Believe it or not, pretending is good for you. The more you *act* like you're happy, confident, and relaxed, the more you'll *feel* like you're happy, confident, and relaxed. In other words, your actions can change your feelings.

How can you act like you're up when you feel down? Start by smiling. And smile with your eyes, not just your mouth. Think about something funny. Read a joke book. Listen to a comedy tape.

You might try reading out loud. Pick something that conveys a pleasant or funny mood, and read with expression. Exaggerate your expressions and voice as you read it.

Dressing up helps too. When you're down in the dumps, pick your loveliest dress or your best looking suit. Looking good makes it easier to feel better about yourself.

DON'T ACT LIKE YOU FEEL; ACT THE WAY YOU WANT TO FEEL.

Our capacity to control our moods is simply amazing. When you're feeling depressed and then act like you're depressed, you reinforce the depressed feeling and actually make yourself feel worse. If you act like you're happy, even though you don't feel that way, your actions begin to change your mood until you begin to feel as happy as you're acting.

The next time you feel down, just act like you're not. Before you know it, you'll be feeling great!

64

CHOOSING THE RIGHT WORD

Do you sometimes get confused over choosing the right word?

According to newscaster Bill Moyers, "The great enemy of understanding is imprecise language. Yet the pollution of our language spreads everywhere, like great globs of sludge crowding the shores of public thought." Now there's a man who knows how to use words!

Whether from ignorance or laziness, many of us are sloppy about the way we use words. For example, almost everyone confuses podium and lectern. A lectern is the pedestal a speaker uses to hold notes. A podium is the elevated platform the speaker stands on. You could properly say, "The speaker requested that a lectern be placed in the center of the podium."

We also often confuse affect and effect. "Affect" means to change, modify, or influence. "Effect" is a result or consequence. "The effect of yesterday's storm will certainly affect the city's budget."

Another example is convince and persuade. "Convince" means to create a belief in something. It must always be followed by "of" or "that." "Persuade" means to talk someone into doing something. For instance, "I am convinced that we need to change our policy, and I hope to persuade the committee to act now."

> "THE GREAT ENEMY OF UNDERSTANDING IS IMPRECISE LANGUAGE."

Consider the words imply and infer. To "imply" is to indicate or suggest without expressly saying so. To "infer" is to conclude by reasoning. For example, "I did not mean to imply what you have inferred."

Another case could be further and farther. "Further" means to a greater extent. "Farther" means a greater distance. For example, "He commutes farther than anyone, and has gone further in his attempt to make commuting time productive."

As Mark Twain pointed out, "The difference between the right word and the almost right word is like the difference between lightning and a lightning bug." Learn a new word everyday. Look up words to check their precise meaning. Improve your vocabulary, and you will improve your understanding at the same time.

65

COPING WITH HOSTILITY

Have you ever had to cope with an angry customer? Did you do so gracefully?

Upset, angry, and even hostile customers are simply a fact of life. No matter what you do, sooner or later you'll face one.

Most of us dread a confrontation with an irate customer. We aren't sure how to respond, and we tend to become as emotionally charged as they are. Before we know it, we're in a yelling contest that has no where to go but down. When that happens, no one wins.

The next time you have to deal with an angry customer, try these 12 tips.

1. Don't take their hostility personally. Try to keep your emotions out of it.

2. Don't try to understand the hostility; instead, focus on coping with it.

3. Don't retaliate in kind. Be quiet, firm, and detached.

4. Don't try to stop the harangue until the person has said everything he wants to say, or until he starts repeating things.

5. Use careful questions to uncover the real problem.

6. Speak gently. The Bible says that a soft answer turns away anger.

7. Don't criticize. Focus on issues, not personalities.

8. Listen carefully. Give the person your full attention.

9. Try to use positive body language and facial expressions.

10. Don't act condescending. Be sincere and empathetic.

UPSET, ANGRY, AND EVEN HOSTILE CUSTOMERS ARE SIMPLY A FACT OF LIFE.

11. If you can resolve the conflict or solve the problem, do so willingly.

12. Don't expect an angry person to like you. Be satisfied if he or she will listen to you, or if you can successfully settle things.

Approach hostility confidently. Don't shrink back in fear. Anger is a normal expression, and entirely appropriate in some situations. Just be ready to handle it.

66

COMPETITION IS GOOD FOR YOU

If your major competitor went out of business, would you consider that good or bad?

Most companies have an annual management conference to review the results of the last year and prepare for the next. Recently in one such meeting, the president of the company said they had lost their major competitor during the past year. He considered that good.

His comment started me thinking. There have been many times over the years when I've wished my competitors would disappear. We may *say* that competition is good, but I doubt that many of us really feel that way. It's more an abstract truth than an emotional reality. I don't think I've ever told my competitors "thank you" for competing against me. Have you? Usually we feel more threatened than thankful.

Yet, it's often our competitors who motivate us to improve. That's certainly true for the company whose management conference I attended. Striving to out-perform their competitors has propelled them to the top of their industry. With their major competitor gone, I wondered who would keep them honed into winning form? Truth is, when we have no competition, most of us get rusty in a hurry.

A top golfer once told me that I'd never be much better than the people I played against. If I wanted to become a better golfer, he said, I should always play against people better than myself.

WE SHOULD THANK GOD FOR STRONG COMPETITORS.

The same principle is true in every part of our life. We think we'd like to operate free of competition, but if we did we wouldn't perform nearly as well. We wouldn't develop as much, and we'd undoubtedly produce less.

I disagree with the president of that firm. Losing a major competitor is not good. We should thank God for strong competitors. Maybe we should even thank our competitors for pushing us beyond our perceived limits and causing us to become better.

67

YOUR EMPHASIS MAKES ALL THE DIFFERENCE

*H*ow you say something is often more important than *what* you say. Words are powerful, and how you use them either harnesses that power for you or unleashes it against you.

For example, a political candidate recently said, "My opponent's background will *not* be an issue in this campaign." Everyone knew he meant exactly the opposite.

Zig Ziglar, a noted motivational speaker, often uses humor to illustrate the power of emphasis. For example, take this sentence: "I didn't say he beat his wife." By changing the emphasis, this sentence can take on several different meanings and implications.

"I didn't say he beat his wife. I *didn't*, say he beat his wife. I didn't *say* he beat his wife. I didn't say *he* beat his wife. I didn't say he *beat* his wife. I didn't say he beat *his* wife. I didn't say he beat his *wife*." Really makes a difference, doesn't it?

The mayor of a Midwestern city, running for re-election, had been making speeches, shaking hands, and kissing babies the way all local politicians do. One afternoon he was the guest of honor at the Women's Garden Club, a very influential group in his city. One of the Club members had her new baby with her — an unbelievably ugly baby. But the mayor, living up to his reputation, neither hesitated nor fumbled. He took one look at the ugly child and said, "Now, *that's* a baby!" The mother beamed, and the mayor went on to be re-elected.

WORDS ARE POWERFUL, AND HOW YOU USE THEM EITHER HARNESSES THAT POWER FOR YOU OR UNLEASHES IT AGAINST YOU.

Pay attention to how you emphasize the words you use. Remember, the right word with the right emphasis at the right time has great power.

68

SEVEN WAYS TO PERSUADE OTHERS

Every day, in one way or another, we all try to get someone else to do what we want them to do. The not-so-wise try to control others, while the wise persuade. We often try to control because we don't know how to persuade.

Controlling others is negative and short-lived. All you need for control is a weapon, a threat. Remove the weapon and you lose control. Persuasion, however, is positive. It requires no weapon, and the effects are long-lasting. Furthermore, persuading others is usually not as difficult as we imagine.

To persuade rather than control, experts suggest emphasizing the strong points, offering additional incentives, or stimulating their thinking. Think about what the other person might want and tie that reward to your request. Consider their personality. Some people will respond to a challenge, while others want an assurance of security.

You also might try to change their perception. There is definitely a relationship between the words you use and the perception that is created. For example, we once found our clients balked at "signing a contract" for our services. Most companies required that all contracts be reviewed by their lawyers, which took more time and money. However, the problem vanished when we changed the label and asked them to "OK a letter of agreement."

Eliminating complexity is another useful tactic. Keep it simple. Increasing complexity will often convince someone not do something.

Put deadlines on offers. For example, "This special price is available only until Saturday."

> THE NOT-SO-WISE TRY TO CONTROL OTHERS, WHILE THE WISE PERSUADE.

Make it easy to act with negative options for non-action. Book clubs use this one. Do nothing, and you get the book. If you don't want it, you must send a card back and tell them not to send it.

Practice these points and you'll find that you have more success in persuading others, and you won't be tempted to use the negative alternative of controlling others.

69

LEARN TO TAKE MORE RISKS

A re you afraid to take a risk? Some of us are frightened of risks and are slow to try new things. Others barge ahead, either unaware of the risk or choosing to ignore it.

Risk is a part of life. The majority of the risks we face are social risks. We're afraid of looking foolish, being wrong, or feeling rejected. When these things happen, they hurt; to avoid potential pain, we play it safe and don't take chances.

If we wish to succeed at anything, however, we can't play it safe all the time. Sooner or later we must take risks, whether we like it or not. It would help, then, if we could learn to face risk positively.

Risk-taking is not an inherent quality. It is something we learn to do. The key is self-confidence, which is built by taking a risk and succeeding. Start small and work up to bigger issues. The more you practice the better you get. You'll also develop good judgment along the way, enabling you to determine which risks are worth taking.

Most successful people are positive risk-takers. Here are four guidelines many of them follow to know which risks to take.

1. Read as much as you can, especially about current events. Most people really don't know much about what's happening in the world. The more you know, the less you fear.

2. Be flexible in your world view. We live in an uncertain world that is constantly changing. Instead of worrying about the changes, think about how you can best adapt to them.

RISK IS A PART OF LIFE.

3. Don't let yourself become too attached to your job, your pet projects, or a particular boss. The more attached you are, the more traumatic it is to detach yourself. Nothing lasts forever, and it helps if you can let go positively.

4. Perfect your personal communication skills: reading, writing, and speaking. Your self-confidence will rise and you'll find you have more opportunities to take calculated risks.

The bottom line is this: In order to learn how to take calculated risks, you must educate yourself, then — just do it! The more you try, the more you'll succeed, and the more confident you'll become, which makes you ready for the next risk-taking opportunity that comes along. Remember, start small and work up to the bigger issues. You'll only be successful if you try. If you don't try, you'll never know.

70

HOW TO TURN A BAD MOOD INTO A GOOD MOOD

Everyone has a bad mood now and then; they are simply a part of life. Sooner or later, the bad mood passes away and life is back to normal. However, if you don't want to wait, there are several things you can do to hasten the switch to a good mood.

For starters, you could laugh. Listen to funny tapes by your favorite comedians. Its hard to feel gloomy while you are laughing. Laughter frees the mind and lightens the soul. Laugh away your bad mood.

Music is also a great mood-changer. Play upbeat music, the kind that makes you feel better. Most of us respond positively to 60-cycle music — music with 60 beats per minute. This kind of

HOW TO TURN A BAD MOOD INTO A GOOD MOOD

music automatically produces a calm, relaxed state. Most 60-cycle music is classical. Compositions by Bach are especially good for chasing away the blues.

Exercise is another way to dissipate a bad mood. Rigorous exercise increases the oxygen level in your brain. Exercise also causes the brain to produce extra endorphins, your body's natural antidepressant hormone.

Getting outside helps promote a good mood as well. Cabin fever is no joke. Staying cooped up inside for too long can depress anyone. Your body and your mind need sunlight and fresh air to function at their best.

Do something fun. Too many of us don't seem to have much fun anymore. Plan it, schedule it — and do whatever it takes to make it happen regularly. Remember the old cliché: "All work and no play makes Jack a dull boy." And when Jack is a dull boy, he is also in a bad mood. Make sure you have enough play time in your life.

THERE ARE SEVERAL THINGS YOU CAN DO TO HASTEN THE SWITCH TO A GOOD MOOD.

Increase your stimulation. Do something creative. Do something silly. Get a massage or a manicure. Get a make-over. Go shopping. Clean up your house or your office. Take a drive.

Eventually, a bad mood will disappear all by itself. However, the right activities can hasten its departure.

71

HOW TO GET OUT OF YOUR RUT

F eeling a little bored? Getting tired of your ho-hum routine? Want a bit more excitement in your life? What you need to do is to break out of your rut.

As a young boy in Kansas I learned a great deal about ruts. We faced them on the country roads after heavy rains. Often you would see three or four different ruts heading up the same muddy road. Some went in a fairly straight line; others zig-zagged from side to side.

I remember a sign nailed on a fence post near our home. It read, "Pick your rut with care — you'll drive in it for a long time." They were not kidding, either. Once you got your car into one rut, it was nearly impossible to change to another.

The basic idea was to pick the rut that would get you where you wanted to go. Trouble was, you couldn't always tell which one was the right rut. A rut that started straight could suddenly swerve into the ditch, and if you picked the wrong one that's where you would wind up.

Life is like that. Our habits become ruts. When we choose our habits we also choose the results that come with those habits, and changing habits is not always easy. It helps to break out of the habit — the rut — before it becomes too deep.

WHEN WE CHOOSE OUR HABITS WE ALSO CHOOSE THE RESULTS THAT COME WITH THOSE HABITS.

Here are several ideas to help you break out of your rut.

Get up earlier. Start your day differently. Take a walk at sunrise. Take a bath instead of a shower. Eat something different for breakfast.

Take a new route to work. Take the bus or train instead of driving. Talk to people instead of reading the paper. Change your lunch hour.

Learn a new language. Read a book to your spouse. Do something to help someone else. Learn to do magic tricks.

To break out of your rut, you must break your normal habit patterns and do something different. Become unpredictable. Baffle your family and friends.

In the immortal words of Auntie Mame, "Life is a banquet, and some poor folks are starving to death."

72

HOW TO COPE WITH INFORMATION ANXIETY

Do you ever feel like you just can't keep up anymore? Are you reluctant to admit you don't understand how to use a computer, how to program your VCR, or how to operate a FAX machine?

The more things change and the more new technology we create, the more people there are who don't understand it. It is embarrassing to say you don't know, so you try to fake it. Soon you begin to think you are the only one who doesn't know.

Relax. You are not the only one and you are not unusual, either. You are simply a victim of information anxiety. It hits us because we feel we should be well-rounded, that we should know about everything.

HOW TO COPE WITH INFORMATION ANXIETY

To help you get past the anxious feelings, here are several points to consider. First, if *you* don't know there are probably many others who also don't know. When you speak up, you will almost always find several people who also wanted to know, but were too timid to ask. Practice saying, "I don't know. I don't understand." The more you say it the more you will learn.

Never let anyone intimidate you for lacking knowledge. Not knowing does not diminish your value as a person. "Uninformed" does not mean "stupid." Often the ones who try to make fun of your ignorance don't know much more than you do. They may have only a little knowledge, but they act as if they know it all.

Develop the habit of learning something new every week. You can learn a great deal over the course of a year. You will never know everything, but you can always learn more. Just recently I've learned how to program numbers into the telephone and how to set the VCR to record while we're gone. In the past few months I have also mastered three new software programs for my computer.

ANXIETY, COUPLED WITH INACTIVITY, BREEDS EVEN MORE ANXIETY.

Anxiety, coupled with inactivity, breeds even more anxiety. You can reduce your anxiety by admitting you lack knowledge, refusing to let the show-offs intimidate you, and striving continually to learn something new.

73

HOW TO BE LESS PERFECT

Perfectionism strikes about 40 percent of us, some to a greater degree than others. At least 20 percent of us are real fuss-budgets. We expect too much of ourselves and place impossible demands on others.

Perfectionists today face a terrible dilemma. On every hand we are told to set our sights higher, to strive for quality, to pursue excellence. For the perfectionist, excellence means perfection. However, perfection is rarely possible.

Perfectionism creates a fear of failure. It causes low self-esteem, procrastination, and nit-picking. Perfectionists often major in minors; they get so involved with trivia they completely miss the larger issues.

Perfectionists have a hard time setting priorities, because everything seems to be equally important. There are no degrees of perfection. They spend far too much time, effort, and money on a job. Ironically, they often miss deadlines. Their jobs and their lives become oppressive, and they suffer burnout much more often than non-perfectionists.

Before seeking psychological counseling, there is much you can do to curb perfectionist behavior. First, try to relax — loosen-up. A Chinese proverb says, "Life is too important to be taken seriously." Learn to laugh, especially at yourself and your foibles.

MANAGERS ARE PAID TO GET RESULTS, NOT TO BE PERFECT.

Work at learning the difference between competency and perfection. Peter Drucker, the famous management consultant, wrote that managers are paid to get results not to be perfect. Strive to do a job well enough to achieve the desired results, and then stop. Don't continue beyond that point seeking perfection.

Change the way you talk to yourself. Stop reciting all the "I shoulds" that occur to you. Most of them are self-imposed, unrealistic standards. Allow yourself to enjoy life like your "imperfect" friends.

Becoming less perfect may be difficult and take some time, but it is worth the effort. Living free from perfectionism will allow you to enjoy life and accomplish much more. You can be very good at your job without being perfect.

74

HOW LIKABLE ARE YOU?

Most of us want people to like us. Life seems better that way. We seldom complain about being liked too much by too many people!

Whether or not others like us is largely up to us. It depends on what we do and how we get along with others. Many of us are not getting along with others as well as we like to pretend.

We say we want others to like us for who we are. That often means we are not doing things we ought to do and we don't intend to change, either. "Why can't they just like me the way I am?" Truth is, to be *liked* we must be *likable*.

Being likable is not all that hard to do. For openers, are you really interested in other people? We seldom like people who act as if they are only interested in themselves. When you meet someone, smile while you talk to them. Convey a friendly attitude. Ask about their concerns. Be understanding and considerate of their feelings.

Greet people as soon as you see them. Don't wait for them to greet you first. Call them by name. Give them the impression that you are genuinely happy to see them.

Act like you enjoy life. Look on the optimistic side of things even when you don't feel like it. Express yourself in positive ways. Don't be a whiner and complainer.

WHETHER OR NOT OTHERS LIKE US IS LARGELY UP TO US.

Never try to make yourself look good by putting others down. Build others up instead of criticizing them. Look for the good in people. Praise others generously, both to their face *and* behind their back.

Be courteous and practice good manners at all times. It takes no more time to be courteous than to be rude, and it pays much better dividends. Be patient, no matter what happens.

If you would like to increase your likability quotient, start practicing all these ideas on a regular basis. When you do, you will find it is not difficult to get other people to like you.

75

WHAT'S YOUR FATAL FLAW?

In Greek mythology Achilles was a mighty warrior. He was practically indestructible. His only flaw was one small spot on his heel. Of course, that's where the arrow hit that brought him down. This myth is the basis of our concept of an Achilles heel — a fatal flaw.

We all have a fatal flaw, or at least a potentially fatal flaw. That is something that, if not covered, will bring us down, something so potent it can overcome all our strengths. The newspapers are full of examples of this every day.

Some argue that flaws aren't that critical. After all, they say, no one is perfect. Yes, that's true, and we should overlook people's weaknesses. A *fatal* flaw, though, can't just be overlooked, and certainly not forever.

The ancient church fathers recognized the problem of fatal flaws. They described seven deadly sins that could cause great damage to body and soul: slothfulness, lust, anger, pride, envy, gluttony, and greed. The church warned to beware the dangers and to strive to control these seven areas. These sins are as damaging today as they were centuries ago.

Fatal flaws can be almost anything: refusing to take advice, rebelling against authority, or opposing change. It might be lying, cheating, stealing, or gossiping.

Here is the main point: Unless you control your fatal flaw, it gets worse over time. It might even start innocently, but then grow out of control.

What can you do? First, if you don't know what your fatal flaw is, find out. Examine yourself with a critical eye . Ask others who know you well.

Second, commit yourself to fixing the flaw. Work on strengthening that area of your life so you are less vulnerable.

UNLESS YOU LEARN TO CONTROL YOUR FATAL FLAW, IT GETS WORSE OVER TIME.

Third, make yourself accountable to someone. Ask them to check up on you. Accountability is critical for conquering fatal flaws.

Fatal flaws need not be fatal. When detected, work to fix them. If you fail to fix them, however, you may wind up in a fix.

76

EIGHT STEPS TO STRONGER SELF-ESTEEM

The stronger your self-esteem, the better your life. Here are eight steps that can help you strengthen your self-esteem.

Step 1: Accept yourself. Ninety percent of Americans are unhappy with the way they look. Yet, most of us will never be ideal. Stop complaining about what you aren't, and learn to accept what you are. Internal qualities are more important than external characteristics.

Step 2: Improve your inner self. The average American spends almost $500 every year to improve their external appearance and less than $10 to improve their mind. Buy fewer clothes and more books. Attend fewer movies and more seminars.

Step 3: Tap your inner joy. Do activities you enjoy, just for the pleasure of the experience. They don't have to lead anywhere, produce an economic pay-off, or enhance your career. Do something for others. Cheerfully giving yourself to others produces great inner joy.

Step 4: Be positive about yourself. Concentrate on what you *can* do, not on what you *can't* do. Keep a praise book to record compliments and praises you get from others. Note anything you do well.

Step 5: Forget about perfection. Life is in the living. If you enjoy baking it doesn't matter if your cake is lopsided. Learn to laugh at yourself.

IN ALL THE UNIVERSE, THERE IS ONLY ONE YOU.

Step 6: Take a chance. The thing people often regret most in life is not taking more risks. Be brave. Step out boldly. To risk is to grow.

Step 7: Learn from others. Pick positive role models who have a great deal of self-esteem. Study them. Notice what they do and how they do it. Look for clues that will help you. Copy some of their good habits.

Step 8: In all the universe, there is only one you. Celebrate your uniqueness! This is your greatest asset. Accentuate your uniqueness. Make it the foundation for greater self-esteem as you continue to grow and develop.

GETTING AHEAD

*What good will it be for a man if he gains
the whole world, yet forfeits his soul?
Matthew 16:26*

77

HOW TO GET PROMOTED

W ould you like a promotion on your job? Most of us would, but we don't always know how to make it happen. Many of us assume that luck is the predominant variable.

In reality, research shows that luck has very little to do with getting a promotion. Instead, studies point to several useful guidelines. The people who get promoted most often consistently use these ideas. Perhaps the things that work for them will work for you too.

Here are six common elements in a successful strategy for getting a promotion.

1. Think about accomplishment, not hours spent. It is not your effort but your results that usually count most.

2. Delegate as much as you can. Let other people help you. You will multiply your efforts and raise everyone's level of achievement.

3. Don't over-plan. It is better to have a general strategy which allows you to change and bend as situations develop. A plan that is too elaborate tends to make you inflexible.

4. Evaluate subordinates honestly, both those who do well and those who perform poorly. Treat everyone fairly and consistently.

5. Promote subordinates' careers, even at the risk of losing good people. When others know you are really trying to help them succeed, they will try to help you succeed.

6. Be positive with people. Don't be negative and critical or take a hard-nosed attitude.

IN REALITY, RESEARCH SHOWS THAT LUCK HAS VERY LITTLE TO DO WITH GETTING A PROMOTION.

Sometimes we make things too hard. These are not big, complicated issues; they are little, ordinary ones. Strive for results, delegate, be flexible, be honest, help others succeed, and be positive. Do these things consistently and you will probably get the promotions you desire.

78

PROFESSIONAL IMPRESSIONS

M ost of us can pick out the real pros with very little effort. Almost everything they do sets them apart as someone special. However, we often don't even have to wait for them to do something to tell who the pros are. We can usually tell before they do or say anything.

What is it that tells us who the pros are? Their walk, their clothes, their expressions, their tone of voice, and the words they choose, especially when they greet us. All of these elements work together to create a positive, professional impression.

Try this test. Go into any store or car dealership and survey the typical salesperson. Which ones really stand out? They are often the ones who send you a nonverbal message that says, "I am a real professional, and you will be glad you met me." Sure enough, when you do meet such a person, you almost automatically like them. You trust them and want to do business with them.

Compare those who create a professional impression with the others. The difference is clear. Their clothes are clean, pressed, and fit well. They dress appropriately; they are not underdressed or overdressed.

They stand straight, shoulders back, chin up, eyes smiling. Their stride is brisk. They don't slump, slouch, or stare at the floor.

Their voices are pleasant, they smile a lot, and they look you in the eye. They are confident without being pushy or arrogant. They choose positive words, statements, or questions. They make you feel at ease.

YOU NEVER GET A SECOND CHANCE TO MAKE A FIRST IMPRESSION.

So here is the question: Do *you* look like a professional? What is your packaging like? What first impression do you create? Sometimes we forget the first impression is often the last impression. Remember, you never get a second chance to make a first impression. Do everything you can to make sure your first impression is a truly professional one.

79

WHY SHOULD SOMEONE HIRE YOU?

Many people are looking for work these days. If you are in that position remember, the basic question is: "Why should we hire you?" Whether you need or want the job has little to do with it.

Many of us approach job interviews with fuzzy assumptions about why people get hired. The most important aspect of a job interview is proving what you can do for the prospective employer and why you can provide that benefit better than anyone else.

Obviously, you need to know something about the company. The more you know, the better. You're looking for the connection between what they need and what you can offer. That alone is not enough, though. To have a really positive interview experience you need to have a good understanding of yourself. What situations do you thrive in? Why? What is the best way to present your strengths during the interview?

Many of us spend too much time learning about the company and not enough time learning about ourselves. This makes it easy to fall into a "facts and figures" trap, while ignoring the dynamics of the interview itself. Don't intimidate the interviewer by reciting reams of data that don't relate to the interview content.

THE BASIC QUESTION IS: "WHY SHOULD WE HIRE YOU?"

Often an interviewer is not looking for specific, factual answers to questions. You're not there to pass a test on company data. The interviewer wants to know how you think, how you formulate your responses, and how you relate things. Underneath it all, the interviewer will be wondering whether or not you have what they need.

The next time you prepare for an interview, go ahead and do your research on the company, but don't forget to do some research on yourself too. Then you'll be ready to answer the question: "Why should we hire you?"

80

ASKING SMART

Would you like a raise? Are you a little nervous about asking for one?

Sonja Hamlin, writing in *Working Woman* magazine, offered some good advice for anyone who feels underpaid. She said, "Ask for a raise; but do it smart."

Asking smart begins with an honest assessment of yourself and your contributions to the company. What impact do you have on profits? Are you doing anything unique? What have been your greatest achievements? What have you improved? How have you been able to save the company money? What new skills have you developed lately?

Hamlin suggests listing the important tasks you handle, as well as special accomplishments. Then prepare a one-page memo outlining and documenting the significant points. This will help you prepare for your request, and it is something you can leave behind for the boss to review after you have made your presentation.

A word of caution: If you can't think of anything noteworthy about yourself or your work, maybe this is not the time to ask for a raise. There might be a problem or two you ought to fix first.

Assuming you can build a good case, don't just barge in and ask for the raise. Practice first. Most of us have some difficulty saying something we have never said before. It might even be a good idea to rehearse with someone else.

Will this strategy work? Hamlin says the boss will usually take one of three approaches. Yes, no, or I'll have to think about it. Thinking it over can also go one of three ways. Yes, no, or compromising for less than you asked for. You need to consider how you will respond to all these conditions.

ASKING SMART BEGINS WITH AN HONEST ASSESSMENT OF YOURSELF AND YOUR CONTRIBUTIONS.

Personal experience tells me there is also a fourth possibility. You might get fired. If that should happen, that company is not the kind you want to work for anyway. Go ahead, ask for a raise. Just be sure to prepare yourself and ask for it smart.

81

HANDLING SUDDEN PROMOTION

Y ou have labored long and hard to be good at your job. Your actions are confident, positive, and decisive. Then suddenly you are promoted into a management position. Your confidence level drops. You are worried, anxious, and indecisive. What happened?

This is a common occurrence. The aggressive salesman becomes a timid sales manager. The confident credit analyst becomes an indecisive loan officer. The relaxed worker becomes an uptight supervisor.

Here are several guidelines which can help you handle a sudden promotion.

First, expect to feel anxious and inadequate. These are normal feelings when you are in a new situation. In fact, this can actually sharpen your mind and increase your energy level. Keep everything in perspective and don't let your fears immobilize you. Talking things out with someone else often helps.

Develop a plan for learning your new job. Ask questions. Listen more than you talk. If you knew everything you needed to know, you would be overqualified. Everyone expects you to learn and grow in your new position. Seek sound advice and competent coaches.

Accentuate the positive. Assess your strengths and weaknesses fairly and then concentrate on your strengths. They are probably the traits that got you the new position. Where you are lacking, seek help. If you are not sure about your strengths, ask your supervisor why you were chosen for the job. Ask trusted colleagues for their perceptions of your strengths.

EVERYONE EXPECTS YOU TO LEARN AND GROW IN YOUR NEW POSITION.

Prepare for discomfort. You may be doing less of the work you were good at and probably enjoyed. You will need to create new habits and routines. You will spend less time doing and more time delegating. All this adds up to initial discomfort during the transition period.

Finally, expect to come out on top. There is an overwhelming tendency to get what you expect.

82

DRIVING THE BOSS CRAZY

You may be sabotaging your chances for success without realizing it. According to Dr. Elior Kinarthy at Rio Hondo College, there are five types of employees who drive bosses crazy. To increase your chances for success it helps to know what to avoid.

Type No. 1: *The Loader-Upper*. These people continually over-commit themselves. They think they can do everything, and do it well too. However, there is a limit to what any of us can do, let alone do well. When we push beyond that limit we often produce poor results, or perhaps no results at all.

Type No. 2: *The Fence Sitter*. These are people who can't make up their mind. They keep collecting more and more information, hoping that the sheer mass of data will make the right decision for them. Unfortunately, this seldom happens. In the meantime, while they are searching for more information, everything is slowed down.

Type No. 3: *The Yo-Yo*. These people constantly jump back and forth from one task to another. They seldom complete anything on time and leave a string of partially completed jobs behind them.

Type No. 4: *The Procrastinator*. If a task is unpleasant or difficult, these people will put it off every time. This creates problems for others as well as for themselves. The longer they wait, the tougher it becomes to produce good results with the project.

Type No. 5: *The Messy Worker*. These people have elevated clutter to an art form. While a little clutter won't hurt anyone, there is a point beyond which it definitely hinders your efforts. All the clutter may also demoralize the workers around them.

YOU MAY BE SABOTAGING YOUR CHANCES FOR SUCCESS WITHOUT REALIZING IT.

One thing clearly emerges from Professor Kinarthy's five classifications. If you fit into one or more of his five types, you will probably have many problems along the way. You probably won't get promoted much, either.

83

FIRING YOUR BOSS

U nfortunately, most of us have had at least one boss who was a dud. We would have fired him or her with glee — if only we could have.

While workers can't actually discharge their bosses in a formal sense, they often fire them informally. When the boss has been "fired," workers do only the minimum necessary tasks. They never volunteer. They don't cooperate. They complain. They file more grievances. They only do exactly what they're told to do. They may even set the boss up or sabotage him so he really *is* discharged.

Workers don't fire good bosses, but they regularly fire poor ones. *Industry Week* magazine once listed twenty of the most likely reasons why workers fire their bosses.

1. Being rude or harsh.

2. Hiring from the outside instead of promoting from within.

3. Breaking promises.

4. Showing favoritism.

5. Practicing discrimination.

6. Ignoring health and safety rules.

7. Criticizing or disciplining with peers present.

8. Paying inequitably.

9. Making frequent changes in rules, hours, or assignments.

10. Withholding praise for good work.

11. Forcing a choice between job and family.

12. Disciplining inconsistently.

13. Substandard wages or benefits.

14. Not listening.

15. Technical incompetence.

16. Ambiguous rules.

17. Dirty, disorganized work place.

18. Slow to give raises.

19. Giving poor instructions.

20. Demonstrating a lack of concern for workers.

WORKERS DON'T FIRE GOOD BOSSES, BUT THEY REGULARLY FIRE POOR ONES.

If you're a manager or likely to become one, this list should make you stop and think. How would your workers rate you?

84

THINGS BOSSES DON'T LIKE

Have you ever wondered what managers dislike most about the people they supervise? A recent study asked managers at all levels that question. Here are their top complaints.

1. Procrastinating instead of acting on things. Do-it-later tendencies are a major source of delays, frustration, and problems for others.

2. Passing the buck. Many of us are unwilling to accept responsibility, make decisions, or admit it when we make mistakes.

3. Claiming to know how to do something and then messing it up. Jobs are often more complicated than they seem. Many of us charge right in without bothering to check carefully. We would do well to remember, "When all else fails, read the instructions.

4. Doing the absolute minimum expected instead of doing the little extra needed to excel. The result is mediocrity for the worker, the department, and the entire firm.

5. Delivering sloppy or unfinished work. It takes extra time and effort to correct deficiencies. When work is late everyone down line feels the pressure.

6. Trying to work beyond our abilities. We all have limitations and it helps if we know where they are.

7. Regularly going over the boss' head. We may win an occasional battle, but we almost always lose the war.

8. Constantly engaging in personal conversation, vicious gossiping, and idle socializing. This one is a bit of a dilemma.

THE WILLINGNESS TO WORK HARD REMAINS ONE OF THE KEY INGREDIENTS FOR SUCCESS.

Personal conversations and socializing are the grease that keeps the organization working smoothly. The key here is balance; striving to keep these things within reasonable limits.

9. Laziness. The willingness to work hard remains one of the key ingredients for success.

What these nine things boil down to is this: If you are going to work for someone, work for them. Pretending to work just won't do.

85

HOW TO SELL YOURSELF BETTER

Everyone knows that before you can sell your ideas, products, or services, you have to sell yourself. The question is: How do you do that best?

To sell yourself is largely a matter of getting other people to like you. If they like you, people will do all kinds of things for you. The advantage is tremendous. They will accept your ideas, buy your products, and follow your lead. However, if they don't like you, they will go out of their way to avoid you.

What is it that makes people like you? That is a tough question. Ask a dozen people and you will probably get a dozen different answers. About the only common link is that most of them will say a pleasant personality is the key.

HOW TO SELL YOURSELF BETTER

In selling yourself, then, begin by showing others you are a pleasant person. To do so, here are five guidelines that will help:

1. Don't boast about yourself or your achievements. Instead, focus on other people and their accomplishments. Let them have the spotlight. Since most people love to talk about themselves they will admire you for listening.

2. Look for something good in everyone you meet. When you find it, comment on it. Sincere compliments are always welcome.

3. Be considerate of everyone no matter who they are. How you treat others, especially those who don't seem to count much, says much about what kind of person you are.

4. Smile often. A smile radiates happiness. Smiles are also contagious. The more you smile, the more everyone else smiles too.

5. Don't volunteer your opinions, especially on sensitive issues. You will avoid many arguments and you will actually find it much easier to convince others of your point-of-view.

TO SELL YOURSELF IS LARGELY A MATTER OF GETTING OTHER PEOPLE TO LIKE YOU.

By following these five guidelines you can go a long way toward successfully selling yourself to other people. Why not start practicing today?

86

THE PURPOSE OF RESUMES

E xactly what *is* the purpose of sending a resume to a prospective employer?

Resumes are a part of the job-seeking process. Whenever you send a resume to someone, its sole purpose is to gain you an interview. However, some people still think their resume alone will determine whether or not they are hired. They pack a detailed life history into their resume, which usually ends up in the wastebasket.

The tendency to include too much information often results from focusing on yourself rather than on the prospective employer. If you focus on yourself, there is a tendency to write a resume that lists all the highlights of your life and says what a great person you are.

THE PURPOSE OF RESUMES

Instead of concentrating on yourself as a person, think of yourself only in relation to the prospective employer. Exactly what can you offer them? Why should they hire you instead of someone else? How do you measure up to what they need? You are not interesting because of what you did in the past. You are interesting because of your potential for doing something valuable for them in the future.

Your resume is really a selling device, not an historical fact sheet. Yes, it will contain many facts about you, but they should be presented in such a way that the reader says, "Here's one that's different. Let's set up an interview and learn more."

REMEMBER YOUR RESUME IS REALLY A SELLING DEVICE, NOT AN HISTORICAL FACT SHEET.

Here are a few tips from the experts. First, be brief and don't repeat yourself. In two or three paragraphs describe what you have done and what you can do. Give the reader the impression that you can do something valuable for his or her company.

Second, don't elaborate on personal information and don't bother with references. Be thoroughly honest. One out of five resumes contains outright lies. Lastly, be neat. First impressions count. Sloppy resumes usually aren't even read.

Remember, a resume is simply a selling tool to get you an interview. A good one is more likely to do just that.

87

INTERVIEW ERRORS

I f you are interviewing for a new job you will significantly improve your chances if you avoid eight deadly errors.

Some people lose a job before they even get it, simply because they handle themselves poorly during the interview. When your chance comes, you will want to put your best foot forward. To help you do that, remember these eight guidelines:

1. Don't try to tell your prospective employer how to run his business. That is not likely to impress him. Be patient and diplomatic. Besides, they must be doing something right if they have a job to offer.

2. Don't criticize your previous company or the people you worked with. Bad-mouthing others doesn't make you look better; it makes you look bad.

3. Don't be unduly modest. Speak up positively about your strong points. Don't brag or boast, just tell it straight and emphasize your contribution.

4. Don't volunteer information about your weaknesses or shortcomings. If you are asked be honest, but don't be too harsh on yourself either.

5. Don't ask about salary or benefits in the first interview. You don't want to risk making the impression that you are more interested in the money than in the work.

6. Don't ask too many questions. Be particularly careful not to put the interviewer on the spot.

7. Don't be late for your appointment. There is never a good enough excuse. B. C. Forbes once observed that he never quite trusted the man who was late. Many employers feel the same way.

8. Don't dress poorly. Dress appropriately for the occasion; not underdressed, and not overdressed.

SOME PEOPLE LOSE A JOB BEFORE THEY EVEN GET IT, SIMPLY BECAUSE THEY HANDLE THEMSELVES POORLY DURING THE INTERVIEW.

Avoiding these eight blunders during an interview can help highlight your positive points and improve your chances of being hired.

88

YOU ARE WHAT YOU WEAR

Does it really matter what you wear? It does if you are a physician. At least that's the conclusion of a study conducted at Harvard Medical School. Dr. Thomas Lee concluded from the research that people want their doctor to look like a doctor. He maintains that people prefer a doctor who looks like he deserves their respect, maybe even their reverence. If you are a physician, the study suggests you would be smart to dress conservatively.

What about the rest of us who are not physicians? Bill Thourlby, one of the pioneer wardrobe consultants, says that you are what you wear. Thourlby claims that others make at least ten decisions about you based solely on your wardrobe. Purely based on how you look, they will decide:

1. Your economic level.
2. Your educational level.
3. Your trustworthiness.
4. Your social position.
5. Your level of sophistication.
6. Your economic heritage.
7. Your social heritage.
8. Your educational heritage.
9. Your level of success.
10. Your moral character.

If people see you favorably, you have a head start toward success in any situation. Thourlby's book, *You Are What You Wear*, offers good advice on how to do that.

IF PEOPLE SEE YOU FAVORABLY, YOU HAVE A HEAD START TOWARD SUCCESS IN ANY SITUATION.

Still some doubt in your mind? The Queen of England once wrote this to her son: "Dress gives one the outward sign from which people in general can and do judge upon the inward state of mind and feelings of a person; for this they can see, while the other they cannot see. On that account, clothes are of particular importance."

Like it or not, agree or not, how you dress is vitally important. As Daniel Webster wrote, "The world is governed more by appearance than by realities, so that it is fully as necessary to seem to know something as it is to know it."

89

TRAINING TRANSFER

W hy is it that so much of our training efforts fail to produce changes on the job? We call it training failure. Just because you've learned a better way to do something doesn't mean you'll actually do it that way.

The point of most training is to improve job performance. When knowledge and skills developed in training classes are not used on the job, the entire training effort is wasted.

Sometimes upper level managers will not accept new techniques taught in a training program. Sometimes we send people to classes to learn things that don't apply to them on their jobs. And sometimes there is no encouragement or help in applying new techniques to actual work assignments.

If there's a large number of people to be trained and very limited training resources, the training program may drag out over a long time period, making implementation very difficult. Perhaps the people assigned to receive the training miss some classes. And some people see training classes as simply a "day off."

Several things must take place in order to make sure training pays off in better job performance. First, do a careful assessment of what kind of training is truly needed and for which people. Second, after the training occurs, the employee must be held accountable for actually using the new skills or knowledge on the job. This means supervisors must encourage the new changes and be helpful and supportive.

WHEN KNOWLEDGE AND SKILLS DEVELOPED IN TRAINING CLASSES ARE NOT USED ON THE JOB, THE ENTIRE TRAINING EFFORT IS WASTED.

Everyone involved must be trained closely together. Then the new techniques must also be practiced by all the managers, starting at the very top. One of the truisms of business is that people tend to work like their managers.

Successful training must be carefully planned, skillfully executed, and persistently followed-up.

SIX TIPS TO IMPROVE YOUR NETWORKING SKILLS

Networking is one the new buzzwords of the 90's. It means developing contacts with people who can help you, buy your products or services, or refer you to others who may buy. The concept, however, is an old one. "It's not *what* you know, but *who* you know."

Tip No. 1: Talk with everyone you meet — in professional meetings, church socials, or even waiting in lines. Show genuine interest. Share comments and concerns in a positive, friendly manner.

Tip No. 2: Be prepared with a short, simple explanation when someone asks what you do. The idea is to increase their interest.

Just a sentence or two will do. A long, confusing explanation dampens their interest. Use simple, ordinary words and avoid technical jargon.

Tip No. 3: Look around for someone who is standing alone. You may find they are feeling awkward and will welcome your approach. They may enjoy a conversation, but be too shy to start one.

Tip No. 4: Keep the conversation going, but don't monopolize it. Your focus should be on building friendships, not trying to sell everyone you meet. Get the other person to talk first. If you really focus on them, you will probably learn a great deal about their needs and concerns.

Tip No. 5: When you are alone, walk up to a group and say, "Hi! I'm new here and don't know anyone. Can I meet all of you?" Most of the time this simple, direct approach works very well.

Tip No. 6: Stay in touch. Meeting someone once is not enough. Send notes, call them, or meet for lunch. Maintain the relationship.

WE ALL PREFER TO DO BUSINESS WITH PEOPLE WE KNOW AND LIKE.

We all prefer to do business with people we know and like. Networking is simply a good way to increase the number of people you know and who know you. Like any skill, the more you practice the better you become.

91

HOW TO GET BETTER RESULTS FROM CONFERENCES

S ome conferences are better than others. However, what you gain from attending a conference depends on how you approach it.

1. Call the speakers ahead of time. Brochures describing the sessions are often ambiguous. Ask speakers for more details about what they will cover.

2. Make a plan for the conference. What do you want to accomplish? What kinds of ideas are you looking for? Which people do you want to meet?

3. Arrive early and meet the speakers. Tell the speakers why you are there and what you hope to gain; they'll often adjust their comments and try to address your needs.

4. Listen attentively. Concentrate on what the speaker is saying. Make sure you understand the points discussed. Write down questions that occur to you so you can ask them at the proper time.

5. Take notes. Write down people's names and other pertinent details. Don't rely on your memory. Write down the ideas which you can use. Personalize your notes. Be specific. Assign action dates.

6. Participate in discussions. Ideas expand when they are discussed. Share your ideas and experiences and encourage others to share their ideas with you.

7. Be patient. Learn to appreciate the other person's point of view. Keep a smile on your face and in your comments.

8. Think positive. Look for the good. Ignore what doesn't apply to you, but don't criticize. Some ideas may work better for you while different ideas may be better for others. Concentrate on thinking of positive ways you can use the ideas.

WHAT YOU GAIN FROM ATTENDING A CONFERENCE DEPENDS ON HOW YOU APPROACH IT.

9. Prepare an action plan. Debrief yourself at the end of the conference. Write out a plan for using what you have learned. Decide exactly what you will do and when you will do it.

Follow up promptly. Procrastination is the worst enemy of new ideas. Take positive action immediately, no matter how small.

92

POSITIVE VISIBILITY BOOSTS YOUR CAREER

Being in the right place at the right time often means gaining a valuable opportunity. I call it positive visibility. Many people assume it is simply a matter of luck. Others know better. I have always liked a definition of luck suggested by Ann Landers: "Luck is when opportunity and preparation meet. It is often disguised as hard work."

If positive visibility is not just luck, then how do you make it happen? Here are several strategies that have worked for many people.

1. Write articles for industry trade journals or your own company magazine. Editors are always looking for good writers who have something worthwhile to say. The more your name appears in print the better your chance for positive visibility.

2. Volunteer to present papers at industry conferences. It takes more effort, but the results can be amazing. One young man leap-frogged three levels to a vice-presidency on the strength of a paper he presented. Was it just luck that the president of the firm happened to be in the audience?

3. Make the most of any opportunity. A great five-minute presentation at a management meeting could do more for you than five years of experience. Be prepared. Rehearse. Dress well. Act like your career hangs in the balance.

4. Learn to network. Go to association meetings, conferences, or alumni functions in your area. Friendships developed are often stronger than you realize. Don't be insincere, but be your most positive self.

5. Polish your speaking and writing skills. Even mundane memos can be a visibility opportunity. An increasing number of people speak and write poorly. Someone who does both well will stand out immediately.

> "LUCK IS WHEN OPPORTUNITY AND PREPARATION MEET. IT IS OFTEN DISGUISED AS HARD WORK."

6. Develop your people skills. Learn to read people accurately and respond appropriately. Discover fresh ways to motivate and persuade others. Be polite and positive. Good people skills are highly visible and long-remembered.

Positive visibility is not a matter of luck, in the traditional sense. It is a result of going the extra mile and doing so with excellence.

93

GOOD WRITING BOOSTS YOUR CAREER

Good writing is increasingly critical in most jobs. Yet according to the experts, the average adult is a poor writer. For instance, most of us use three to five times more words than necessary to say what we have to say.

Here are several guidelines which can help you use fewer words, say more, and say it better.

1. Keep sentences short — no more than 15-20 words. Long sentences are hard to understand and slow to read.

2. Use the active voice. Most business writing uses the passive voice, which requires 30-50 percent more words.

3. Use simple, ordinary words. Avoid big words, fancy phrases, technical jargon, and worn-out clichés.

4. Keep paragraphs short. In most cases, three or four sentences per paragraph is plenty.

5. Identify the exact result you want before you start. What do you hope to achieve with your letter, memo, or report?

6. Make an outline. What is the best way to achieve your intended result? Think first, write second.

7. Edit, edit, edit. Do it yourself or ask someone to do it for you. Try one of the new computer programs like Grammatik. It checks your writing against various rules for good writing.

8. Write like you talk. People who could tell you something clearly and concisely often write obscurely.

9. Get a good style manual. My preference is *Elements of Style*, by William Strunk and E. B. White. First published in 1929, it is still the best 71 pages available on good writing. Practice using their principles.

GOOD WRITING WILL NOT HAPPEN AUTOMATIC- ALLY; YOU MUST WORK AT IT.

The rewards for good writing are increasing. While you may never win a Pulitzer Prize, you can easily enhance your career. Good writing will not happen automatically; you must work at it. The good news, though, is that anyone can learn to be a better writer.

MANAGING BETTER

*What is this thing you are doing? Why do
you alone sit as judge? What you are doing
is not good...you cannot handle it alone.*
Exodus 18:14–18

94

SEVEN STEPS FOR BETTER DELEGATING

"If you want it done right, you have to do it yourself." Everywhere you go, people are having difficulty with delegation.

Some of the failure comes from a lack of understanding about what delegation is. It's much more than just assigning work to someone. Delegating means granting someone authority within a specific area of responsibility and holding them accountable. Authority is the right to act and make decisions. Unfortunately, authority also carries with it the right to make mistakes.

Good delegation involves trust. You must trust the other person to tackle what you have delegated, do their best, keep you informed, and let you know when a problem arises. On the other hand, the person you've delegated to has to trust you too. They must trust that you will provide any training needed, give them support, help them when necessary (but not interfere), and give them the credit they deserve. No wonder delegation is so difficult.

There are seven steps for good delegating.

1. Think first. Plan out what you intend to do. This is probably the most neglected step. Don't try to wing it.

2. Clarify the exact responsibility and what results you expect.

3. Select the right person. Sometimes you should pick the person who needs to be developed most, not necessarily the one you can trust the most now.

4. Grant them enough authority to do the job right.

5. Decide how you will control their progress. You want to avoid both over-control and under-control. Tell them how and when you will check on their work. Help them when they need it, but don't breathe down their neck.

6. Give them the job in a motivating manner. Do everything you can to get them off to a positive start.

7. Hold them accountable for their performance.

Follow these seven steps and you will almost certainly do a better job of delegating in the future.

DELEGATING MEANS GRANTING SOMEONE AUTHORITY WITHIN A SPECIFIC AREA OF RESPONSIBILITY AND HOLDING THEM ACCOUNTABLE.

95

BAD BOSSES

I f you supervise others, would you say you're a good boss? Would your employees agree?

The manager-employee relationship is one of the key factors in your success or failure as a boss. Good bosses facilitate greater development, better performance, and positive morale. Poor bosses create negative morale, diminish performance, and literally make people sick.

Dr. Mark Tager, quoted in *Executive Fitness* newsletter, says poor managers may be the most overlooked source of job stress. According to Dr. Tager, the management style of your boss has a powerful effect on your mental, physical, and emotional health.

Through his research, Dr. Tager found four things that seem to characterize bad bosses.

1. They are unpredictable. You never know what mood they will

be in or how they will respond to things. They are not consistent in what they praise or criticize.

2. They tear down self-esteem. They humiliate, ridicule, and disparage employees. They never praise good work or give recognition when it is deserved. They steal credit for what others have done.

3. They create win-lose situations. If the boss wins, then the employees have to lose, or vice-versa. They never look for ways where both can win.

4. They provide too much or too little stimulation. They are insensitive to individual differences in people and are unable, or unwilling, to adjust to those differences.

No wonder people hate to work for this kind of boss. It would be almost impossible to create or maintain a positive, productive environment around such a person.

Please note: This is more than just a work issue. These behaviors would also make you a bad parent, a lousy friend, and a poor colleague. You would be the loser everywhere you go, not just at work.

THE MANAGEMENT STYLE OF YOUR BOSS HAS A POWERFUL EFFECT ON YOUR MENTAL, PHYSICAL, AND EMOTIONAL HEALTH.

If you find yourself fitting into one of these categories, begin working toward positive change today. Your employees will appreciate your efforts.

96

GOOD BOSSES HAVE GOOD PERKS

Being a good boss requires more than just *not* being a bad boss. Dr. Mark Tager, who has studied both good and bad bosses, says there are four characteristics commonly associated with the bad ones. They are unpredictable, diminish other's self-esteem, create win-lose situations, and are insensitive to the varying needs of people. Avoiding these characteristics would keep you from being a bad boss, but would not necessarily make you a good boss.

Dr. Tager, in an interview with *Executive Fitness* newsletter, says there are five things that can help you become a good boss. Just think of PERKS — participation, environment, recognition, knowledge, and skills.

Participation creates a sense of belonging, of being valued. Being valued leads to greater commitment and more care and concern about the job. To foster greater participation, Dr. Tager suggests we listen more. He also advises us to involve employees in decisions and help them set goals for their work.

A positive, supportive environment encourages people to learn, to grow, to try something new. Such an environment requires mutual trust and respect. To increase trust and respect, Dr. Tager suggests being tactful and not blaming others. He also suggests promoting from within and showing appreciation for each person's unique contribution.

Positive feedback is the key to recognition that will increase self-worth. Let people know how they are doing. Give more positive messages than negative ones. Dr. Tager says to give at least four times as many positive messages as negative ones.

Knowledge improves performance. At a minimum, people need to know four things: 1) What you expect them to do; 2) How well you expect them to do it; 3) What resources they have to do it with; and 4) How you will evaluate their performance.

Finally, to promote good relationships, learn to be sensitive to the differences in people. Adjust yourself and the work environment to match their needs.

THERE ARE FIVE THINGS THAT CAN HELP YOU BECOME A GOOD BOSS — PARTICIPATION, ENVIRONMENT, RECOGNITION, KNOWLEDGE, AND SKILLS.

Remember PERKS. They can help you become a good boss.

SUCCESS SECRETS

97

UPWARD DELEGATION

I f you're a manager, do you know how to recognize and prevent upward delegation?

Upward delegation occurs when your subordinates shift their work to you. Consultant Bill Oncken called this a monkey-on-the-back condition. The key to avoiding the condition is to keep the monkeys where they belong.

Suppose you're walking down the hall one day and you meet Tom, one of your subordinates. You say, "Good morning, Tom," and he says, "Hi, boss. Glad I bumped into you. You see, we've got a problem and...." As Tom goes on you realize you know enough to get involved, but not enough to make a decision on the spot. So you say, "Look, Tom, I'm in a hurry right now. Let me think it over, and I'll get back to you."

UPWARD DELEGATION

Bingo! The monkey just jumped from Tom's back to yours. Tom has successfully delegated the problem upward. A couple of days later he'll drop by your office to say, "Hi, boss. About that problem we discussed...how's it coming?" This is called supervisory follow-up. Trouble is, it's going in the wrong direction.

Oncken said the reason subordinates can delegate upward so easily is both the manager and subordinate mistakenly assume the matter under consideration is a joint problem. Whenever a subordinate says, "We have a problem," it's time for extra caution on your part. That "we" may signal a monkey poised to jump from his back to yours.

UPWARD DELEGATION OCCURS WHEN YOUR SUBORDINATES SHIFT THEIR WORK TO YOU.

Your job as a manager is to help your subordinates become good problem solvers. You cannot accomplish that when you're solving their problems for them. In fact, if their problem becomes your problem, they will no longer have a problem; and how can you help someone who doesn't have a problem?

The next time someone comes to see you with a problem, make sure they take the monkey with them when they leave. Offer a suggestion of how they can solve the problem, but make it clear that the problem is theirs to solve. You will both be better off.

98

WHAT WORKERS WANT MOST

Which of the following items would you say are most important to people at work? A good salary? Job security? Appreciation for a job well done? A chance to use your mind and abilities? Medical and other benefits? Being able to retire early with a good pension? A clean, comfortable place to work?

According to a survey by Lou Harris and Associates, the top ranking items were salary, security, appreciation, challenge, benefits, pension, and comfort. The two top concerns, salary and security, are no big surprise. But the third one, appreciation, was unexpected.

If appreciation is so desired and costs so little, why don't we express it more? One factory supervisor told me that in 33 years he had never once expressed appreciation to anyone who had worked for him. I challenged him to begin doing so.

At first he was clumsy and people were suspicious. But once he improved and people discovered he was sincere, surprising things began to happen. People smiled more, helped each other, tried harder, took the initiative, talked nicer to each other, and voluntarily took on extra work. The supervisor could hardly believe it! So much return from such little effort.

> IF APPRECIATION IS SO DESIRED AND COSTS SO LITTLE, WHY DON'T WE EXPRESS IT MORE?

If you would like to add a new dimension to your life, try this experiment. For the next month, tell one person every day what you appreciate about them. Don't force it, just begin noticing and thinking about the positive points of the people around you. Then, tell them what you appreciate most. Do it simply, sincerely, and regularly. After one month, assess whether or not it has made any significant difference in your life.

99

MOTIVATING OTHERS

Deciding on the best way to motivate others is often difficult. When we are trying to motivate others, many of us fall into a trap without realizing it.

For many managers, motivating people is the toughest part of their job. Half of the time, most managers are just guessing. Sometimes things turn out right; sometimes they don't.

Most of us are motivated in similar ways. However, this may be more deceiving than helpful. Although our list of motivators may be similar, the degree to which those things motivate us may be very different. The item on the top of your list could be on the bottom of my list.

Most of us attempt to motivate others the way we prefer to be motivated ourselves. That assumes that what works for me will work for you. If the other person is like you, the results will probably be good. However, if the other person is not like you, this approach could be a big mistake.

Parents with two or more children learn this quickly. The second child is often motivated by different things than the first child. To motivate the second child, parents must observe their children closely and analyze the differences between them.

It works the same way for managers. The difference is that parents often take the time and effort to study the differences between their children. Managers, on the other hand, either can't or won't do that for their employees. It is easier to assume that what works for one should work for all.

MOST OF US ATTEMPT TO MOTIVATE OTHERS THE WAY WE PREFER TO BE MOTIVATED OURSELVES.

Instead of considering what would motivate you, concentrate on the other person. Don't assume anything. Study that person. What would they prefer? Instead of assuming that every person will respond about the same, study the differences between them. The more you understand about the people you are trying to motivate, the better you can motivate them.

100

SIX STEPS FOR IMPROVING WORK FLOW

Peter Drucker, the noted management consultant, once wrote, "So much of what we call management consists of making it difficult for people to work." This is especially true as companies reorganize or downsize. With enough people, the work gets done regardless of inefficiency. These days, however, management levels are disappearing and staffs are growing leaner. Here are six steps to help you manage smarter and improve your results.

Step 1: Be sure everyone knows what to do. Lean organizations cannot afford to wander around aimlessly. Focus all resources on critical issues. Spend even more time clarifying goals and priorities.

SIX STEPS FOR IMPROVING WORKFLOW

Step 2: Examine all rules closely. Many rules grow from management paranoia, excessive ego, and turf-building. Eliminate all rules that hamper performance.

Step 3: Analyze all procedures in detail. Almost any process can be improved. Cut out any unnecessary steps. Delegate authority to lower levels to speed up decisions. Do away with redundant cross-checking and multiple authorizations. One company shortened a key process from 120 days to 4 simply by bypassing several layers of management.

Step 4: Eliminate duplication. Analyze all forms and reports. Many reports are redundant. Half of the files most companies keep are duplications. Different departments may be keeping similar records. Question whether or not you really need every piece of paper.

Step 5: Simplify the work. Strive for fewer stages, tasks, and rules. Work for less movement and faster responses. Identify bottlenecks and eliminate them. Ask the people doing the work for ideas on streamlining the process.

"SO MUCH OF WHAT WE CALL MANAGEMENT CONSISTS OF MAKING IT DIFFICULT FOR PEOPLE TO WORK."

Step 6: Improve supplier relationships. This applies to both internal and external suppliers. Conflicts between engineering and production are as harmful as receiving substandard materials from a supplier. The phrase, "lean and mean" is bad advice. "Lean and friendly" will produce better results.

101

FOLLOW-UP IS CRITICAL FOR SUCCESS

Forgetting to follow-up is a major time waster. We can get so busy we lose track of the details, yet persistent follow-up is a powerful ingredient for success in any field. Here is an example that illustrates this point.

Carl, a friend of mine, visited a local car dealer to see the new models. When he arrived, he saw several salesmen standing around. One of them walked over to help him. He looked at several models and decided on what options and color he wanted. Carl really was in the market for a new car, but he hesitated to spend the money. He told the salesman he would think about it.

Two months later Carl had still not returned to the dealership and he had not heard anything from the salesman.

One day he stopped at another car dealer. When he drove up, a salesman came running across the lot and asked how he could help. They negotiated for awhile, but didn't conclude anything. The next day he received a note from the salesman thanking him for coming in. He said that since they had settled on a particular car, they just needed to reach an agreement on the price. He also said he hoped Carl would return soon.

Carl did go back, but they didn't reach an agreement. The salesman wrote again and followed-up with a phone call, asking him to come back again, which Carl did. The salesman was gracious, pleasant, helpful, businesslike, courteous, and persistent.

PERSISTENT FOLLOW-UP IS A POWERFUL INGREDIENT FOR SUCCESS IN ANY FIELD.

Carl eventually bought the car from this persistent salesman. However, he did even more than that. He also sent him several other prospects, some of whom also bought cars. The second salesman clearly understood the value of persistent follow-up.

When you are writing out your plans for the day or week, don't forget to plan follow-up activities. Be sure to allow enough time in your plans to carry them out. This is one thing that can make a big difference in your results.

102

SPRING CLEANING

Every year at Springtime is the traditional "spring cleaning" time. It's a time to throw open the windows, chase out the dog, and really clean the place from top to bottom. However, when the time comes many of us are intimidated by the size of the job. How do we get started?

Whether at home or the office, there comes a time when we must pause and clean out the junk. It may not be fun, but it can be easier. Here is how.

1. Prepare your family or your staff. Make a plan for your cleaning project. Tell everyone what you are planning, how you are going to do it, and what you expect from them.

2. Get several big boxes. Label them: THROW OUT, PUT SOMEWHERE ELSE, GARAGE SALE, GIVE AWAY, and STORAGE. When a box is full, take it where it belongs and get an empty one.

3. Work each room in a definite pattern. Try clockwise or counter-clockwise, whichever you prefer. Keep the boxes with you. Deal with each and every item as you come to it.

4. Set time limits for each room. Reward yourself for finishing within the time limit.

5. To help decide whether or not to keep something, ask yourself these questions. "Do I like it?" "Do I use it?" "Do I need it?" 'Do I want it?"

6. Group similar things together and store them in one place. Pick a convenient spot. Consider how often they are used and who uses them.

7. Give every person a special memento box. Let them use it for sentimental keepsakes.

8. Learn to enjoy empty space instead of feeling nervous about it. There doesn't have to be something on every shelf.

WHETHER AT HOME OR AT THE OFFICE, THERE COMES A TIME WHEN WE MUST PAUSE AND CLEAN OUT THE JUNK.

Try these ideas and see if spring cleaning doesn't seem so overwhelming. It might even be fun!

103

SMILE ON THE PHONE

Telephone manners can either keep or lose customers. Recent studies show that 70 percent of customers who stopped doing business with a company stopped because of how they were treated on the telephone.

Many people answering the telephone project a negative image. Some sound bored. Some are rude. Some sound angry. Some are in a hurry. Some don't seem to care who you are or why you called. What is really frightening, though, is that you and I are often the culprits.

There is an interesting exhibit in the Chicago Museum of Science and Industry. Two telephones were placed on opposite sides of a large column, so you can talk to another person without seeing each other. The unusual part, is that mirrors are mounted above each telephone. The idea is to smile at yourself in the mirror and see what difference it makes in your voice on the other end of the line.

You don't have to go to Chicago to try this for yourself. Get a mirror and a tape recorder. Call someone and tape your conversation. Talk normally, then smile warmly at yourself in the mirror. As you play the tape back, you will easily hear the improvement in your voice.

Most of us view the telephone as a nuisance. Whenever the phone rings it is an interruption — an intrusion — even though it may be a customer. Whether consciously or not, the caller picks up your attitude. Because the phone is a relatively impersonal instrument, we are not always fully aware of the living, breathing person on the other end. They are often only a voice.

What we say and how we say it are critical issues for telephone etiquette. Put a mirror at every telephone in your office. Encourage everyone to smile at themselves in the mirror while they talk. A smile on your face puts a smile in your voice, and that is a positive step toward better customer relations.

SEVENTY PERCENT OF CUSTOMERS WHO STOPPED DOING BUSINESS WITH A COMPANY STOPPED BECAUSE OF HOW THEY WERE TREATED ON THE TELEPHONE.

104

WRITING CLEAR INSTRUCTIONS

I once bought my girls a little playhouse. When I got it home, I was as excited as they were. We tore open the box, eager to put it together, but the instructions were poorly written and confusing. "What dummy wrote this?" I fumed.

Writing clear instructions can be much easier if you follow these ten steps found in *Teach* newsletter:

1. Prepare the reader. Define the task and list all the equipment needed.

2. Use familiar terms. The person who needs instructions probably won't understand a specialized vocabulary. Stick to simple language.

3. List the steps in chronological order. Be sure the instructions give the steps in proper sequence.

4. Give all necessary warnings. Explain conditions under which an operation should *not* be performed. For instance, "CAUTION: If you smell gas, do not strike the match."

5. Relate the unknown to the known. Compare the new task to one that's familiar to the reader: For instance, "Grasp the first chopstick as you would a pencil."

6. Offer reassurance. Insert occasional phrases that tell the reader he's doing it right. For instance, "The light should now be green."

7. Explain why. Tell the reader why a step is being taken to help him understand the process and complete the step accurately.

8. Use an easy-to-follow format. Number the steps so the reader can focus on one step at a time and easily find the next step.

9. Include drawings or diagrams. Make sure they are properly labeled.

10. Try out instructions. Have someone not familiar with the item try to follow the instructions so you can discover where they are confusing or unclear.

> HAVE SOMEONE NOT FAMILIAR WITH THE ITEM TRY TO FOLLOW THE INSTRUCTIONS SO YOU CAN DISCOVER WHERE THEY ARE CONFUSING OR UNCLEAR.

Try these ten steps the next time you have to write instructions, and you'll probably do a good job.

105

ARE YOU AN EFFECTIVE COMMUNICATOR?

When you step in front of a group are you an effective communicator? Would your audience call you a top presenter?

Whether teaching a class, leading a business meeting, or making a speech, you must do everything you can to hold the listener's attention and get your point across.

Zig Ziglar is one of the top professional speakers in America. He is also an excellent writer and a sparkling conversationalist. In his book, *Top Performance*, Ziglar lists ten guidelines for becoming an effective communicator.

1. Appearance: How you look has an impact on others. Be sure your appearance produces a positive effect.

2. Posture: Stand straight. Sit straight. Walk confidently. Use body language that's consistent with your words.

3. Gestures: Do whatever comes naturally to you, but be sure to do something. Gestures actually help you express yourself better.

4. Eye contact: Your eyes are extremely expressive. Positive thoughts will help you send positive signals.

5. Facial expressions: Use expressions appropriate for what you're saying to help you set the tone of your message.

6. Voice: Vary your pitch, volume, inflection, and pace. As your voice changes, people pay more attention.

7. Involvement: Engage your audience. Ask questions. Use their names. Talk about their interests.

8. Questions: Handle them well. Listen carefully and think before responding.

9. Humor: Used wisely, humor will help others relax and become more friendly and open to your ideas.

BEING AN EFFECTIVE COMMUNICATOR IS MUCH MORE THAN JUST TALKING.

10. Visual aids: Pictures are often more effective than words. Plus, whenever your audience is looking as well as listening, you're more likely to hold their attention.

Being an effective communicator is much more than just talking. If you correctly use all ten of these points, Zig Ziglar says you can make a positive impression on any group.

106

JOB SATISFACTION FACTORS

W hat is it that makes people feel satisfied with their job?

Management consultant Roy Walters has spent years studying job satisfaction and productivity. From his research, he developed a Satisfaction Potential checklist. According to Walters, there are nine characteristics that define a truly satisfying job:

1. The job isn't monotonous, but allows workers to change pace by varying tasks.

2. The job does not waste a person's time and effort. It has been planned in such a way that it can be done without exerting energy uselessly.

3. Workers are free to plan their work the way they can do it most effectively.

4. Workers believe they have a reasonable degree of authority over how their work should be done.

5. Workers believe they have opportunities for individual recognition and growth.

6. Workers don't feel too closely supervised, over-instructed, or rigidly controlled.

7. Workers see their job as an integral part of the whole company and each worker is treated as an individual, not merely a cog in the wheel.

8. The answer to the question, "How am I doing?" comes from the job itself. Thus, workers can correct their own errors and improve their techniques.

9. Superiors offer feedback without causing embarrassment.

THERE ARE NINE CHARACTER-ISTICS THAT DEFINE A JOB THAT IS TRULY SATISFYING.

Wouldn't it be great if every job matched these nine criteria? Can you imagine what effect that would have on the people doing the work? Why not start with the jobs in your own company and see just how satisfying you can make them?

107

NEW MOTIVATIONAL STRATEGIES

Today's worker is different. Old motivational strategies don't work as well as they used to. Today's workers have more affluence, better education, and greater expectations. They place more value on intrinsic rewards and often define success more in terms of personal goals than simply climbing the corporate ladder. The lures of money and promotion just don't work as well with this group.

Dr. Gary Schuman, writing in *Management Solutions* magazine, suggested nine new motivational strategies:

1. Assign an experienced pro to mentor a less experienced person.

2. Cross train people on each other's functional duties to allow alternating job tasks.

3. Provide rotating job assignments to different positions or departments to allow people to broaden their skills.

4. Assign people to various teams to broaden their contacts and expand their ability to work well with different kinds of people.

5. Give special assignments that allow for personal growth and development.

6. Allow the opportunity to develop creative or innovative ways for handling assignments.

7 Give assignments that are personally interesting, or those that provide high visibility.

8. Talk with people about skills they'd like to develop and then look for appropriate learning experiences.

TODAY'S WORKERS HAVE MORE AFFLUENCE, BETTER EDUCATION, AND GREATER EXPECTATIONS.

9. Take people to lunch to provide specific feedback on their performance. Ask how they feel about what's happening and what assignments they find interesting.

108

IMPROVING COMMUNICATIONS

I f you wanted to improve the way people communicate with each other, how would you go about it? What would you do?

Mountain Bell once asked people what they thought they needed for improved communication. The answers are still as valid as ever. Here are the suggestions people offered:

1. Share important information first thing in the morning, before people get involved with other projects.

2. Get information out quickly, before rumors spread and dilute the impact of your message. Even if you don't have all the facts yet, you'll still build credibility.

3. Stress benefits. Tell people how something will affect them.

4. If it's controversial, don't be afraid to present opposing

viewpoints. People can be trusted to think and they appreciate your confidence.

5. Don't overload them with information. The majority of us find 15-30 minutes at a time is most comfortable. If more needs to be said, bring it out in a question-and-answer session.

6 Bring in experts to handle subjects you're not comfortable with.

7. Ask managers at all levels to help spread the word within the company. It makes the information more personal, palatable, and more time-effective.

8. Follow up communications with reinforcing materials and information. Repetition is the key to retention.

9. If you're uncomfortable talking in front of groups, seek training. A poor presentation will cause your credibility to suffer.

ASK PEOPLE WHAT THEY WANT TO KNOW AND HOW THEY'D LIKE TO HEAR IT.

10. Don't think of disseminating information strictly as a mass audience proposition. You can also present your message in one-on-one meetings through drop-in visits, coffee breaks, or lunches.

Ask people what they want to know and how they'd like to hear it. Being an effective communicator requires being a good listener. Employees will be more apt to hear what you have to say when you've been willing to hear what they have to say.

109

HOW TO TELL WHEN SOMEONE IS LYING

Experts say we all lie more than we realize. Furthermore, the more often we tell the same lie, the more we forget it is a lie. If we repeat it enough, we may even believe the lie is actually the truth.

According to the experts who study lying, there are several clues to watch for to determine if someone is lying to you. First, when someone is telling a prepared lie they often give unusually brief answers or answer too quickly. Their responses may sound rehearsed. After responding they may nod their head, scratch their body, or rub their hands together.

Second, spontaneous liars also give very brief answers, pause much more than usual, and avoid any discussion of details. They make lots of false starts and reverse direction in their responses. They also make more grammatical errors and use broad terms like "all" or "always."

The more we tell a particular lie, the better we get at it. A lie is easiest to detect the first time it is told. If we know that what we are saying is a lie, our behavior changes. When we lie, our behavior is often at odds with our words. This is true for both spontaneous and prepared lies.

WHEN WE LIE, OUR BEHAVIOR IS OFTEN AT ODDS WITH OUR WORDS.

As we grow older we become better liars. Young children are usually forthrightly honest, sometimes to their parents' embarrassment. However, by the time they are 8 to 10 years old, most children can lie as skillfully as adults, usually displaying the same behavioral clues as adults.

According to the experts, more people are lying and they are lying more often. If this is true, we must become adept at spotting the clues. It can be useful to know when someone is lying.

SUCCESS SECRETS

110

BUILDING TRUST

Trust is a critical foundation for good relationships. Friendships, families, and organizations need trust to operate effectively. When we trust one another, everything works better. But trust isn't automatic; we must earn it.

Some people earn trust quickly. Their attitudes and behaviors make it easy for others to trust them.

Strong trust builders keep their promises, whether to their clients, colleagues, or children. You can rely on them to do what they said they would do.

They tell the truth, even when it may be painful or to their disadvantage.

When they do something wrong they are quick to apologize. They sincerely regret wronging others.

They are good listeners. They listen at least as much as they talk.

They praise people generously. They are constantly watching for what others do right and comment on it.

They willingly cooperate with their colleagues. They are more interested in achieving good results than in who gets the credit.

They strive to understand how others feel. They are sensitive and empathetic.

They look out for other people's interests as well as their own.

They are fair in their dealings with everyone.

They clarify their intentions so others will understand their actions.

They seek input on all issues from the people who will be affected by their decisions or actions.

Strong trust builders are extremely relationship-oriented. They really care about others. They actively practice the Golden Rule, treating others the way they would want to be treated.

FRIENDSHIPS, FAMILIES, AND ORGANIZATIONS NEED TRUST TO OPERATE EFFECTIVELY.

When you demonstrate these attitudes and behaviors people just naturally trust you. They trust you faster too. They enjoy working, or living, with you.

111

HOW TO MAKE VOICE MAIL CUSTOMER FRIENDLY

A sk people about voice mail and you'll uncover both love and hate. Whether or not people will like your voice mail system lies in how well you set it up.

Unfortunately, many companies are making serious mistakes in using voice mail. All too often, voice mail is set up primarily for the convenience of the company. Customer reaction is apparently not considered. Here are several guidelines that can help make your voice mail a positive asset.

1. Answer the phone on the first or second ring.

2. Test messages with real customers. Find out what they like and dislike.

3. Use a real person to record the message. Avoid using machine-like computer voices. People like to hear people.

4. Keep messages short and simple.

5. Don't give more than two or three choices at a time.

6. Always give callers the option of talking to a live person. Do this early in the message. For example, you might let the caller decide whether to leave a message in the voice mail box or talk to a secretary.

7. Use ordinary language. Avoid computer jargon or abbreviations known only to insiders.

8. Give callers a choice between waiting and holding. If you offer to call them back promptly, be sure to do so.

9. Don't try to deliver complex, detailed information in the message.

10. Give the number after the instruction, not before. For example, "For customer service, press 1."

11. Make sure the message is clear, distinct, and spoken at a moderate speed.

WHETHER OR NOT PEOPLE WILL LIKE YOUR VOICE MAIL SYSTEMS LIES IN HOW WELL YOU SET IT UP.

12. Give callers the option of hearing instructions a second time, or as many times as they like.

Many people are unfamiliar and uncomfortable with voice mail. A customer-friendly system will help win them over and make them feel at ease.

112

THREE STEPS FOR BEING A SUPER SUPERVISOR

D o you really enjoy supervising others? Two out of three supervisors asked this question said no. Why? Most said they don't like supervising others because they don't know how to do it well. When asked to explain further, they said the problem stemmed more from human relations issues than from technical issues.

Dr. Kim McKinnon, writing in *Management Solutions*, suggested a three-step approach based on sound behavioral research. Dr. McKinnon calls it the TOP model. TOP is an acronym for the three steps.

THREE STEPS FOR BEING A SUPER SUPERVISOR

Step 1: T — Tell them what you expect. Results depend on expectations. Most people try to do what you expect of them. Tell them what you want and you'll probably get it.

Step 2: O — Observe their performance. Observing is not as easy as it sounds. It involves more than just watching now and then. The key is frequent observation at different times and in different situations. Keep detailed notes so you won't forget what you've observed.

Step 3: P — Provide meaningful feedback. Good feedback requires making specific comments. Telling someone their performance is good or poor is meaningless unless you can refer to specific examples. Use praise when performance meets or exceeds what you expect. Use problem-solving feedback when performance falls short.

TELLING SOMEONE THEIR PERFORMANCE IS GOOD OR POOR IS MEANINGLESS UNLESS YOU CAN REFER TO SPECIFIC EXAMPLES.

The TOP model is simple. Tell them what you expect, observe their performance, and provide meaningful feedback.

If you use this approach consistently, you'll find that the people you supervise will accomplish more. Then, when you see that your new supervision style leads to greater results, you'll feel much better and more confident about supervising others.

MANAGING STRESS

The Lord is my shepherd, I shall not
be in want.
He makes me lie down in green pastures,
he leads
me beside quiet waters, he restores my soul.
Psalm 23:1-2

113

BURNOUT SYMPTOMS

Have you ever noticed the label on a spray can? It says, "CAUTION: Contents under pressure." Many of us are like that. There's a lot of pressure on the inside. We sometimes feel like we're going to explode. We're fatigued, bored, depressed, cynical, irritable, impatient, and maybe even paranoid. Yet there's no particular problem or crisis we can point to. These negative feelings may be due to burnout.

Many psychologists describe burnout as fatigue or frustration brought about by devotion to a cause, way of life, or relationship that failed to produce the expected reward. The main thing they all emphasize is that something must be done — and the sooner the better.

Believe it or not, more work can help, not hurt. Instead of quitting your job, you might just add another one that's challenging and enjoyable. Moonlighting can lift your spirits and give you a fresh perspective on your regular job.

Vigorous exercise can also help overcome the symptoms of burnout. Exercise can nourish both body and soul. Your overall fitness will increase and your body chemistry will improve. More and more people are turning to rigorous exercise programs to help readjust themselves.

Altering your daily routine is also a good idea. Even something as simple as driving a new route to work or changing your lunch hour can be beneficial.

Learning to relax is essential. Burnout victims usually feel uptight most of the time. You might try deep muscle relaxation techniques or try changing the way you see yourself in relation to your world.

MAKING EVEN ONE SMALL CHANGE CAN CREATE A SIGNIFICANT IMPROVEMENT IN YOUR MENTAL WELL-BEING.

Learning to say no both to yourself and others will probably help. You don't have to respond to every demand or pursue every opportunity.

The point is, there are quite a few things you can do to counter burnout. All of them can be beneficial. You don't have to be a victim. Making even one small change can create a significant improvement in your mental well-being.

114

COMMON SENSE WAYS TO BATTLE BURNOUT

Do you sometimes feel overwhelmed by too much to do? Are events scheduled too tightly? Does the pace get too fast? If so, the burnout monster may be hovering over your shoulder. Here are several simple techniques that can help you shoo him away.

1. Slow down your work pace. Delay jobs that are not critical. Allow yourself more time to finish. Don't take on anything new until you complete the jobs you have.

2. Adjust your schedule. Change the timing or duration of certain activities. Get up earlier or later. Variety, remember, is the spice of life.

3. Get more sleep. Many people keep up with their busy lives by cutting back on sleep. The cost may be higher than you realize. Too little sleep not only hinders your performance, but it also affects the way you think.

4. Ask for help. Delegate tasks to others. Ironically, people are often more willing to help than you are to ask.

5. Take a break. Walking around the block or a weekend vacation can do wonders. Get away from your work both physically and mentally.

6. Slow down your living pace. Think "relaxed." Linger over meals. Walk slower, talk slower, think slower. Go to a movie. Sit in the park. Go for a drive in the country. Take a nap.

PEOPLE ARE OFTEN MORE WILLING TO HELP THAN YOU ARE TO ASK.

7. Watch your diet. When you are feeling burned out your body is experiencing stress too. The greater the stress you are under, the more nutrients you need. Eat a balanced diet. Ease up on the caffeine.

8. Exercise more. Take a brisk walk every day. Go to the gym regularly. Chop wood. Clean house. Exercise helps your body fight off the effects of stress and helps clear your mind.

Don't wait until burnout has you all tied up. It's good, common sense to watch for the early warning signs and move quickly to block those burned-out feelings.

115

MANAGING STRESS

Do you have any idea what stress-related illness costs each year? Recent estimates place the annual cost of stress between 50 and 75 billion dollars. Obviously stress is a significant problem that affects many of us, directly or indirectly.

Stress is part of life. Even under the best conditions you can experience stress. The key to handling it is to develop a plan for managing stress daily. You can't pop a pill now and then and make it go away. Instead, you need to change the way you live and how you respond to events in your life.

What people call "stress" is a set of emotional and physical responses to the things happening in their lives. Effective strategies for managing stress, therefore, must consider both physical and emotional conditions.

Regular exercise and good nutrition help combat the physical effects of stress. Regular exercise means three or four times a week. It should stretch your body and elevate your heart rate for at least 20 minutes. Common examples include walking, jogging, or bicycling.

Good nutrition means a well-balanced diet, eating moderate quantities, limiting caffeine, and maintaining proper vitamin levels. It also helps to discontinue harmful habits, such as smoking.

Combating the emotional part of stress calls for relaxation. Relaxing allows you to release fear and frustration, clearing your mind of tense or troubling thoughts. This can be done in many ways, such as laughing, praying, meditating, sleeping, listening to music, or reading.

Stressful emotions are also relieved when you control your time and priorities. Controlling time and priorities includes defining your goals, planning activities, avoiding over-commitment, and realizing that no one can do everything.

Yes, your stress can be managed, but you must have a sensible plan for achieving it.

WHAT PEOPLE CALL "STRESS" IS A SET OF EMOTIONAL AND PHYSICAL RESPONSES TO THE THINGS HAPPENING IN THEIR LIVES.

116

WHICH EXERCISE IS BEST FOR REDUCING STRESS?

Successfully coping with stress requires good physical and mental health habits. One key aspect is exercise. You need to exercise three or four times weekly, stretching the body and elevating the heart rate.

Once you decide to do it, how do you choose the exercise that will work best for you? Professor Jessica Jenner of Clark University suggests using the COPE formula, which is an acronym for control, opportunity, pleasure, and ease.

Control is the freedom to do an activity whenever and wherever you choose. Opportunity considers any barriers to access. Pleasure relates to your level of personal enjoyment. And ease is how well you can fit the activity in with all the other demands on your time.

WHICH EXERCISE IS BEST FOR REDUCING STRESS?

For example, you might be considering either golf or walking as ways to exercise more. In terms of control, walking is better. You can't play golf whenever and wherever you choose.

On the opportunity scale, walking scores best again. You don't need anything special in terms of facilities or equipment, just a good pair of shoes. Golf however, is weather dependent, and it requires expensive equipment and access to a golf course.

On the pleasure side, golf may score higher than walking. In terms of ease, again, walking outscores golf. It is far easier to fit a walk into your daily schedule than to fit in a round of golf.

Again, for exercise to be beneficial, it needs to be done three or four times weekly, stretch the body, and elevate the heart rate. Walking can easily qualify; golf probably won't — certainly not three or four times a week.

Professor Jenner suggests any exercise that ranks low on two or more of the COPE criteria is not a good choice for a primary exercise. Therefore, golf would be out, but walking would be a good choice for a regular exercise program. Golf might be a good choice for a secondary exercise, or occasional relaxation.

SUCCESSFULLY COPING WITH STRESS REQUIRES GOOD PHYSICAL AND MENTAL HEALTH HABITS.

Professor Jenner's COPE formula can be a good way to help you develop an effective exercise strategy for coping with stress. Remember: Control, Opportunity, Pleasure, and Ease.

117

DON'T BE IN SUCH A HURRY!

Are you a rushaholic? Always in a hurry?

We all know one and some of us are one. Continually on the go. Never relaxed. Always doing something. Compulsive fast-trackers. Forever taking on more and more commitments. Walk fast, talk fast, eat fast — and some say die fast too.

There are many different reasons why people become rushaholics. Some feel the hectic, over-scheduled approach is the best way to get ahead. Constantly trying to balance three things at once makes them feel they are really accomplishing something. However, much of what they do is often trivial, and they never seem to have time to develop good relationships. Over the long run they may do more things but actually accomplish less.

DON'T BE IN SUCH A HURRY!

Some who rush around ceaselessly are trying to hurry life along. Never content with the present, they dream about the ideal tomorrow which, of course, never arrives. Research reveals that many rushaholics may suffer from insecurity or low self-esteem. Taking on more and more is their attempt to make themselves feel worthwhile.

If you would like to slow down, here are several ideas that may help. Start by changing your expectations. You don't have to do everything. Say no more often, especially to yourself. Stop and think before you automatically say yes to the requests of others. Build quiet time into your life. Slow down. Deliberately walk slower, eat slower, talk slower, and drive slower. Practice being patient. Remind yourself that you can't buy love and respect with constant activity.

YOU CAN'T BUY LOVE AND RESPECT WITH CONSTANT ACTIVITY.

When you are rushing all the time, it is difficult to enjoy living. Why not relax a bit? If you do, you will probably discover that while you are doing less, you are actually accomplishing more.

MEET THE AUTHOR

Dr. Merrill Douglass is a speaker, consultant, and author. He is also a man on a mission. His goal is to change the way people think, work, and live — to help them achieve more productive results and more positive relationships — to achieve greater productivity, increased satisfaction, and a better quality of life.

Since 1972, Dr. Douglass has become an internationally recognized authority on time management and personal productivity. He has presented over 2000 programs and seminars in 36 countries around the world. His clients have included Fortune 500 firms, government agencies, leading universities, trade associations, church organizations, and small- to medium-sized businesses of all kinds. In 1976, Dr. Douglass created the deluxe two-day Time Management seminar for the American Management Association, which has become the premiere program of its kind in the US. He has presented this program over 600 times since 1976.

There have been many awards along the way. The National Speakers Association named him a Certified Speaking Professional in 1983. He received the Sammy Award in Research and Development for creating the unique *Time Mastery Profile*. *Fortune Magazine* and *The Wall Street Journal* have called him a top expert. He has been listed in *Who's Who in America*, *American Men and Women of Science*, *Who's Who in Finance and Industry*, and *Personalities of the South*.

Dr. Douglass is the author of several books, including *Manage Your Time Your Work Yourself* and *Time Management for Teams*. His books have been translated into five languages. His cassette tape album, *The New Time Management*, was a best-seller. Dr. Douglass has also written hundreds of articles for magazines and journals, newspaper columns, and daily radio commentaries. The essays in this book were taken from his syndicated column, *Success Secrets*.

In his consulting and seminar work, Dr. Douglass draws upon a varied background in business and education. He has many years of practical experience as a successful manager and entrepreneur, and has also been a professor at several universities. He earned his doctorate from Indiana University, with a double-major in Management and Organizational Behavior.

For more information about seminars, consulting services, or to write the author, please send your correspondence to:

Dr. Merrill Douglass
1401 Johnson Ferry Road, Suite 328
Marietta, GA 30062
770-973-3977 (Tel)
770-973-4603 (Fax)

Additional copies of this
title are available from
your local bookstore.

Honor Books
Tulsa, Oklahoma